School House

to

White House

THE EDUCATION OF THE PRESIDENTS

FROM THE HOLDINGS
OF THE NATIONAL ARCHIVES
PRESIDENTIAL LIBRARIES

The Foundation for the National Archives, Washington DC
in association with D Giles Limited, London

Copyright © 2007 The Foundation for the National Archives
First published in 2007 by GILES
an imprint of D Giles Limited
2nd Floor,
162-164 Upper Richmond Road,
London, SW15 2SL, UK
www.gilesltd.com

This book is based on the exhibition "School House to White House: The Education of the Presidents," presented at the National Archives, Washington, DC, in the Lawrence F. O'Brien Gallery from March 30, 2007, to January 1, 2008. Over the subsequent two years a traveling version of "School House to White House" is planned to visit Presidential Libraries across the nation.

Library of Congress Cataloging-in-Publication Data

School house to White House : the education of the presidents.
    p. cm.
"Based on an exhibition in the Lawrence F. O'Brien Gallery at the National Archives."
ISBN 978-1-904832-43-0 (hardcover) – ISBN 978-0-9758601-4-4 (softcover)
1. Presidents–Education–United States–Exhibitions. 2. Presidents–United States–Biography–Exhibitions. 3. Presidents–United States–History–20th century Exhibitions. 4. Presidents–United States–History–21st century–Exhibitions. 5. Political leadership–United States–Exhibitions. 6. United States–Politics and government–1929-1933–Exhibitions. 7. United States–Politics and government–1933-1945–Exhibitions. 8. United States–Politics and government–1945-1989–Exhibitions. 9. United States–Politics and government–1989–Exhibitions. I. Foundation for the National Archives.
    E176.1.S3523 2007
    973.09'9--dc22
        2007007372

ISBN (softcover): 978-0-9758601-4-4
ISBN (hardcover): 978-1-904832-43-0

For the Foundation for the National Archives:
Thora Colot, Executive Director
Christina Gehring, Publications and Research Manager

For GILES:
Proofread by Moira Johnston
Designed by Anikst Design, London
Produced by the Publisher, an imprint of D Giles Limited
Printed and bound in China

Photographic Credits
The majority of items reproduced in this book are from the holdings of the National Archives System of Presidential Libraries, which unless otherwise noted, supplied the photographs.

Front cover: Montage of Presidents as schoolchildren. Standing from left to right (back row): Franklin D. Roosevelt, Lyndon B. Johnson, Herbert Hoover, and Ronald Reagan; standing from left to right (front row) George W. Bush, Jimmy Carter, John F. Kennedy, and Dwight D. Eisenhower.

Table of Contents

I am pleased to present *School House to White House: The Education of the Presidents*, a book outlining the educational experiences of our modern Presidents beginning with Herbert Hoover. Here the holdings of the National Archives and Records Administration's (NARA) Presidential Libraries tell a story of scholarship, leadership, and participation in school that helped shape the lives of future Presidents—individuals from diverse backgrounds whose education laid the early groundwork to a range of service in the highest elective office in the land.

This is the story of the education of American leaders although the pages of this book also reveal something else: commonalities between the experiences of young future Presidents and one's own experiences growing and learning in grade school, high school, or college. Just like the rest of us, our modern Presidents were once children and young adults studying, participating in extracurricular activities, and considering career paths. Their story offers important insight into our present situation and raises questions about the education for our future leaders.

Most of the images presented in this book depict documents and artifacts preserved in NARA's Presidential Libraries. These are not typical libraries with books to check out. Rather, these institutions are archives and museums that preserve the written records and physical history of our Presidents while providing special programs and exhibits that serve their communities. They belong to the American people and provide to the public insight into the times in which these Presidents lived and served the nation.

The release of this book coincides with the opening of the exhibit "School House to White House: The Education of the Presidents." The exhibit and book together represent a collaboration among archival and museum staffs of the Presidential Libraries and the Center for the National Archives Experience as well as the support of the Foundation for the National Archives. The exhibit first opened in the National Archives Building in Washington, DC, and then at select Presidential Libraries across the country and includes education and public programs that enhance the visitor's experience. The book, available at NARA gift stores nationwide, will reach many members of the public who have not had the opportunity to visit the exhibit. Coordinating NARA's vast resources in this way supports a significant goal of NARA's strategic plan: increasing access to our records in ways that further civic literacy in America through our museums, public outreach, and education programs.

While attending Stanford as part of the university's first class, Herbert Hoover served as manager of the baseball team and was responsible for collecting admission fees for home games. During one game former President Benjamin Harrison, who was lecturing at Stanford, accidentally gained admission without paying for a ticket. Future-President Hoover caught up with the former President and politely asked for the admission fee which was quickly paid. Hoover said it was "My first contact with a great public man."

Like President Hoover, many of us have had experiences in school that have provided foundations and opportunities for our future lives. Utilizing historical records preserved by the National Archives and its system of Presidential Libraries, this book is an opportunity both to learn about our leaders' educations and to reflect on our own experiences growing up.

Allen Weinstein
Archivist of the United States

Acknowledgements

This book *School House to White House: The Education of the Presidents* and the exhibit upon which it is based were created through a collaboration among the professional archival and museum staffs of the National Archives 12 Presidential Libraries and the Center for the National Archives Experience in Washington, DC, as well as staff from the Office of Presidential Libraries, the National Archives Special Media Preservation Laboratory, and the Foundation for the National Archives.

THE FOLLOWING IS A LIST OF THESE IMPORTANT CONTRIBUTORS:

From the Presidential Libraries:

Olivia S. Anastasiadis
Karen Anson
Laurie Austin
Kim Barbieri
Clay Bauske
Adam Bergfeld
Mark Beveridge
Steve Branch
Patricia Burchfield
Bonnie Burlbaw
Debbie Carter
Racheal Carter
Stephen Charla
Erik Christman
Bob Clark
Brooke Clement
Josh Cochran
Greg Cumming
Bettina Demetz
Jim Detlefsen
Susan Donius
James Draper
Mike Duggan
Herman Eberhardt
Marcus Ekhardt

Jennifer Evans
Mary Evans
Mary Finch
Michelle Frauenberger
Ray Geselbracht
Renee Gravois
Maryrose Grossman
Marlon Guinn
Ken Hafeli
Elizabeth Hansen
Maureen Harding
Margaret Harman
Nancy Hassett
Kelly Hendren
Donald Holloway
Dan Holt
Spencer Howard
Ben Irwin
John Keller
Sharon Kelly
Tammy Kelly
Cynthia Koch
Michelle Kopfer
James Kratsas
Barbara Kurata
Meghan Lee

9

Donna Lehman
Jim Leyerzapf
Michael MacDonald
Bill McNitt
Mary Ann McSweeney
Dennis Medina
Christine Mickey
Nancy Mirshah
Tim Morales
Chris Mouw
Nathan Myers
Sylvia Naguib
Audra Oliver
Jay Patton
Jennifer Pedersen
Ira Pemstein
Edward Quick
Mark Renovitch
Scott Roley
Matt Schaefer
Lynn Smith
David Stanhope
Dwight Strandberg
Kathy Struss
Pauline Testerman
Alycia Vivona
Tim Walch
Melissa Walker
Karl Weissenbach
Amy Williams
Ray Wilson

From the Center for the National Archives Experience:
Catherine Farmer
Christina Hardman
Karen Hibbitt
Jennifer Nichols Johnson
Darlene McClurkin
Tom Nastick

Marvin Pinkert
Ray Ruskin
Christina Rudy Smith
Maria Stanwich
James Zeender

From the National Archives Special Media Preservation Laboratory:
Steve Puglia
Jeffrey Reed

From the Foundation for the National Archives:
Bruce Banks
Thora Colot
Franck Cordes
Christina Gehring
Stefanie Mathew
Tibbett Speer

Maureen MacDonald from NARA's Product Development Staff was the exhibit project editor.

The exhibit was coordinated by Jennifer Nichols Johnson and designed by Ray Ruskin. The exhibit script was written by Sharon L. Barry.

Special thanks are extended to Ben Irwin and Christina Gehring for their efforts on the development of this publication.

About the Presidential Library System

The Presidential Library system is made up of 12 Presidential Libraries. This nationwide network of libraries is administered by the Office of Presidential Libraries, which is part of the National Archives and Records Administration (NARA), located in College Park, Maryland. These are not traditional libraries, but rather repositories for preserving and making available the papers, records, and other historical materials of U.S. Presidents since Herbert Hoover. Each Presidential Library contains a museum and provides an active series of education and public programs. When a President leaves office, NARA establishes a Presidential project until a new Presidential Library is built and transferred to the Government.

The Presidential Library system formally began in 1939, when President Franklin Roosevelt donated his personal and Presidential papers to the Federal Government. At the same time, Roosevelt pledged part of his estate at Hyde Park to the United States, and friends of the President formed a nonprofit corporation to raise funds for the construction of the library and museum building. Roosevelt's decision stemmed from a firm belief that Presidential papers are an important part of the national heritage and should be accessible to the public. He asked the National Archives to take custody of his papers and other historical materials and to administer his library. At the dedication of his library on June 30, 1941, Franklin Roosevelt observed:

To bring together the records of the past and to house them in buildings where they will be preserved for the use of men and women in the future, a Nation must believe in three things.

It must believe in the past.
It must believe in the future.
It must, above all, believe in the capacity of its own people so to learn from the past that they can gain in judgment in creating their own future.

THE NATIONAL ARCHIVES
PRESIDENTIAL LIBRARIES

Office of Presidential Libraries
National Archives at College Park
8601 Adelphi Road
College Park, MD 20740-6001
301-837-3250
F: 301-837-3199
W: www.archives.gov/presidential-
libraries/

Herbert Hoover Presidential Library
210 Parkside Drive, P.O. Box 488
West Branch, IA 52358-0488
319-643-5301
F: 319-643-6045
E: hoover.library@nara.gov
W: http://hoover.archives.gov

Franklin D. Roosevelt Presidential
Library
4079 Albany Post Road
Hyde Park, NY 12538-1999
1-800-FDR-VISIT or 845-486-7770
F: 845-486-1147
E: roosevelt.library@nara.gov
W: www.fdrlibrary.marist.edu

Harry S. Truman Presidential
Library
500 West U.S. Highway 24
Independence, MO 64050-1798
816-268-8200
F: 816-268-8295
E: truman.library@nara.gov
W: www.trumanlibrary.org

Dwight D. Eisenhower Presidential
Library
200 Southeast Fourth Street
Abilene, KS 67410-2900
785-263-4751
F: 785-263-6718
E: eisenhower.library@nara.gov
W: www.eisenhower.archives.gov

John Fitzgerald Kennedy
Presidential Library
Columbia Point
Boston, MA 02125-3398
877-616-4599 (toll free) or
617-514-1600
F: 617-514-1652
E: kennedy.library@nara.gov
W: www.jfklibrary.org

Lyndon Baines Johnson Presidential
Library
2313 Red River Street
Austin, TX 78705-5702
512-721-0200
F: 512-721-0170
E: johnson.library@nara.gov
W: www.lbjlib.utexas.edu

Richard Nixon Presidential Library
18001 Yorba Linda Boulevard
Yorba Linda, CA 92886
714-983-9120
F: 714-983-9111
E: nixon@nara.gov
W: www.nixon.archives.gov

Gerald R. Ford Presidential
Library and Museum

Gerald R. Ford Library
1000 Beal Avenue
Ann Arbor, MI 48109-2114
734-205-0555
F: 734-205-0571
E: ford.library@nara.gov
W: www.fordlibrarymuseum.gov

Gerald R. Ford Museum
303 Pearl Street, NW
Grand Rapids, MI 49504-5353
616-254-0400
F: 616-254-0386
E: ford.museum@nara.gov
W: www.fordlibrarymuseum.gov

Jimmy Carter Presidential Library
441 Freedom Parkway
Atlanta, GA 30307-1498
404-865-7100
F: 404-865-7102
E: carterlibrary@nara.gov
W: www.jimmycarterlibrary.gov

Ronald Reagan Presidential Library
40 Presidential Drive
Simi Valley, CA 93065-0699
800-410-8354 or 805-577-4000
F: 805-577-4074
E: reagan.library@nara.gov
W: www.reagan.utexas.edu

George H.W. Bush Presidential
Library
1000 George Bush Drive, West
College Station, TX 77845
979-691-4000
F: 979-691-4050
E: bush.library@nara.gov
W: www.bushlibrary.tamu.edu

William J. Clinton Presidential
Library
1200 President Clinton Avenue
Little Rock, AR 72201
501-244-2887
F: 501-244-2883
E: clinton.library@nara.gov
W: www.clinton.library.gov

Presidential Materials Staff
National Archives and Records
Administration
700 Pennsylvania Avenue, NW
Washington, DC 20408-0001
202-357-5200
F: 202-357-5939

Introduction

In 230 years, fewer than 45 people have become President of the United States. Before achieving the highest office in the land, each of these exceptional Americans was once a boy struggling with his studies, a teenager trying to fit in, and a young man choosing a career path. Like many Americans, Presidents once competed for a spot on the football team or a place in their school's band. The challenges of studying various subjects, completing homework, forming new ideas, participating in extracurricular activities, and making friends are part of the common heritage of an American education shared by everyone—including our Presidents.

This book presents the story of the education of the 20th-century Presidents by exploring the holdings of the National Archives system of Presidential Libraries—documents, artifacts, and photographs kept for each President from Herbert Hoover to Bill Clinton. These are not libraries in the usual sense, but rather archives and museums that bring together in one place the materials of a President and his administration and present them to the public for study and discussion without regard for political considerations or affiliations. President Ronald Reagan once described Presidential Libraries as "classrooms of democracy." Here, the holdings of the Libraries illustrate what our leaders accomplished in the classrooms of their youth.

These modern Presidents came from diverse backgrounds, and their educations reflect these differences. Some of the Presidents attended neighborhood public schools, and some of them learned in rural classrooms; others studied under tutors and attended prestigious private schools. Many of the Presidents participated in extracurricular activities and organized sports while they attended school. Although the Presidents examined in this book were good students, an occasional poor grade did appear on a report card. As it is for most of us, education in school and related activities were influential to future Presidents and provided a foundation on which they built the rest of their lives.

This book is an invitation to explore Presidential schooldays through the collections of the National Archives system of Presidential Libraries. Learning about our leaders' lives in school provides for new connections to and perspectives on the Presidency and those who have served as President. It is also an opportunity to reflect on one's own experiences growing up and learning about the world. The school bell is ringing, and everyone has a desk. It's time to go back to school. The Presidents are expecting you.

Home

"*My mother read these to me before
I could read, but I took keen joy
in them for many later years.*"

Franklin D. Roosevelt's
inscription in a companion volume

below
The Great Panjandrum Himself by
Samuel Foote
Franklin D. Roosevelt Presidential
Library and Museum

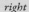

right
Jimmy Carter playing with his pony, Lady Lee, ca. 1931
Jimmy Carter Presidential Library and Museum

middle
Franklin D. Roosevelt, about 14 years old, Germany, 1896
Franklin D. Roosevelt Presidential Library and Museum

bottom
Herbert Hoover (center) with his brother Theodore and sister Mary, West Branch, Iowa, ca. 1881
Herbert Hoover Presidential Library and Museum

For the Presidents, success in school began at home. Whether having stories read to them before bed or checking out books from the library over the summer, these young men grew up in homes that furthered their education. Their parents were often supportive, providing opportunities to learn and an environment to explore interests. For example, Franklin Roosevelt's mother, Sara Delano Roosevelt, closely supervised his education. In addition to arranging for tutors, taking him on educational trips abroad, and encouraging his collecting hobbies, Sara read regularly to young Franklin. *The Great Panjandrum Himself* by Samuel Foote, a popular 18th-century nonsense story, and other children's books are part of Roosevelt's personal book collection of some 17,000 volumes at the Roosevelt Library.

Home

Authors treasured in high school could emerge to impact the President later in life. In April 1901, 16-year-old Harry Truman bought *Idylls of the King* by Alfred, Lord Tennyson. He marked a passage in which a knight tells his mother that he's now a man and must find his destiny. " 'Follow the Christ, the King,' " he says. " 'Live pure, speak true, right wrong, follow the King. / Else, wherefore born?' " Attracted to Tennyson's broad idealism, Truman always carried a handwritten fragment of Tennyson's poem, "Locksley Hall."

above
***Idylls of the King* by Alfred, Lord Tennyson**
Harry S. Truman Presidential Library and Museum

Jimmy Carter wrote in his autobiography, "My life was heavily influenced by our school superintendent, Miss Julia Coleman, who encouraged me to learn about music, art, and especially literature. . . . She encouraged all of her students to seek cultural knowledge beyond the requirements of a normal rural school classroom." Miss Coleman obtained a one-year grant from the Works Progress Administration (WPA) in 1940 to keep the library open for the summer and used the slogan "Readers Make Leaders" to encourage reading.

The home also provided a place to practice new activities. Richard Nixon learned to play the violin, clarinet, saxophone, piano, and the accordion. When he was 12, Richard was sent to live and study music with his mother's sister in central California for six months. His love of music continued throughout his life.

left
Richard Nixon, age 15, holding his violin, 1928
Records of the U.S. Information Agency, National Archives, Courtesy of AP/ Wide World Photos

below
Wood violin
Courtesy of the Richard Nixon Library and Birthplace

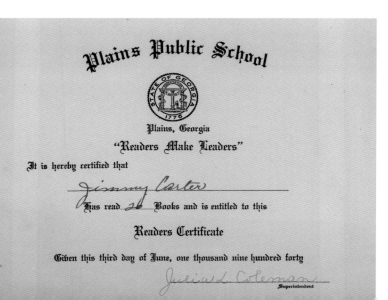

left
"Readers Make Leaders" certificate, Plains Public School, June 3, 1940
Jimmy Carter Presidential Library and Museum

Home

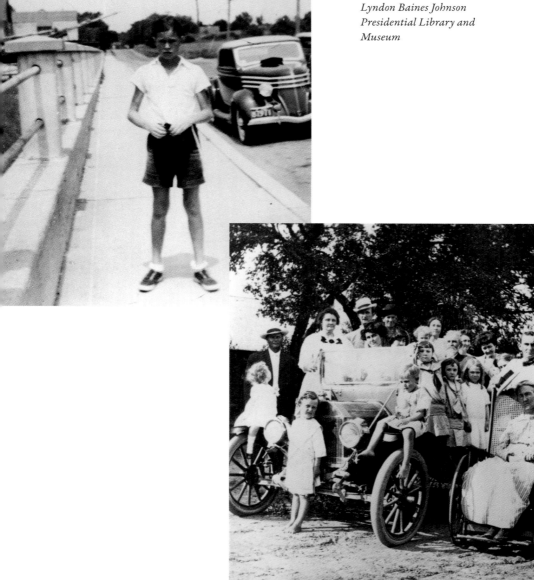

left
**George H.W. Bush,
approximately age 12,
ca. 1936**
*George H.W. Bush Presidential
Library and Museum*

below
**Lyndon B. Johnson
(in front of the automobile),
age 4, and his family, near
Stonewall, Texas, ca. 1912**
*Lyndon Baines Johnson
Presidential Library and
Museum*

above
Harry S. Truman (second from left) and members of his family in a farm wagon, Grandview, Missouri, ca. 1911
Harry S. Truman Presidential Library and Museum

left
Gerald R. Ford, on bike, with cousin Gardner James (left) and two unidentified girls in front of his first home, 1960 Terrace, in Grand Rapids, Michigan, ca. 1915
Gerald R. Ford Presidential Library and Museum

Grade School

"In grammar school, spelling was probably my favorite subject either because the contest aroused my competitive instincts or because I had learned that a single letter could make a vast difference in the meaning of a word."

Dwight D. Eisenhower

left
Jimmy Carter's sixth grade report card, Plains High School, Plains, Georgia, 1935–36
Jimmy Carter Presidential Library and Museum

below
Jimmy Carter's fourth grade geography test, Plains High School, Plains, Georgia, ca. 1933
Jimmy Carter Presidential Library and Museum

REPORT OF

Carter, Jimmy

MONTHS	1	2	3	4	Ex	Av	5	6	7	8	9	Ex	Av	Y. av
DAYS PRESENT	20	20	20	20		80	20	20	20	20			80	160
TIMES TARDY	1	0	0	0		1		1	1				2	3
CONDUCT	a	a	a	a		a	a	a	a	a			a	a
SPELLING	a	a	a	a		a	a	a	a	a			a	a
READING	a	a	a	a		a	a	a	a	a			a	a
WRITING	a	a	a	a		a	a	a	a	a			a	a
ARITHMETIC	a	a	a	a		a	a	a	a	a			a	a
GRAMMAR	B	a	a	a		a	a	a	a	a			a	a
LANGUAGE													a	
GEOGRAPHY	a	a	a	a		a								a } a
HISTORY							a	a	a	a			a	a
HEALTH	a	a	a	a		a	a	a	a	a			a	a
DRAWING														
MUSIC	a	a	a	a		a	a	B	a	C			B	a
AGRICULTURE														

Teeth

Parents please examine, sign and

1 J.E.Carter   2
3 J.E.Carter
5 J.E.Carter   6
7 J.E.Carter   8
9

Geography Les

Jimmy Carter

I name 3 states tha
and vegetables ear
1. California
2. Texas
3. Florida

From their very first day of school, whether in a one-room schoolhouse, neighborhood school, or a private academy, the future Presidents discovered a new, larger world full of facts, figures, and ideas. Many Presidents learned lessons from their teachers that they would remember for the rest of their lives. While in school, a few future Presidents had to overcome the extraordinary challenges of illness, poverty, or the deaths of parents or siblings. Whether their experiences were reflective of their times and communities or were universal to American schooling, they helped mold the characters of these boys who grew up to be President.

Ronald Reagan (second row, far left, with hand on his chin), fourth grade class photo, Tampico, Illinois, 1920
Ronald Reagan Presidential Library and Museum

Grade School

2

Grade School

left
**Dwight D. Eisenhower
(front row, second from
left), fifth grade class,
Lincoln Elementary
School, Abilene, Kansas,
1900**
*Dwight D. Eisenhower
Presidential Library and
Museum*

About his years in school,
Dwight Eisenhower later wrote:
"At one point a suggestion was
made that I should 'skip' a grade.
This is not tribute to any
academic mastery. I suspect that
it was simply recognition that I
lived in a home where learning
was put into practice.... The
suggestion that I skip a grade was
never put into effect. My conduct
was not the equal of my reading
ability."

above
**Herbert Hoover (front
row, far right side) with
classmates, about 11 years
old, Oregon, 1885**
*Herbert Hoover Presidential
Library and Museum*

Harry Truman's only surviving report card has puzzled his biographers. His teacher wrote on the card that it was for second grade, but Truman later remembered that he was in fourth grade this year.

They were probably both right. The report card indicates he started the 1894–95 year in class "A," which was the third term of second grade. He probably skipped a term, or possibly two terms, and by year's end was in the fourth grade.

An example of Harry Truman's homework is "Courage" (1899), an essay from his eighth grade English theme book. He wrote this essay when he was about 15 years old. In it he states a preference for a quiet kind of courage to the more traditional active heroism. He concludes his essay with an outburst of idealism: "A true heart[,] a strong mind[,] and a great deal of courage and I think a man will get through the world."

above

Harry S. Truman's second grade report card, Columbian School, Independence, Missouri, 1894
Harry S. Truman Presidential Library and Museum

below

"Courage," an essay from Harry S. Truman's eighth grade English book.
Courtesy of Martha Ann Swoyer

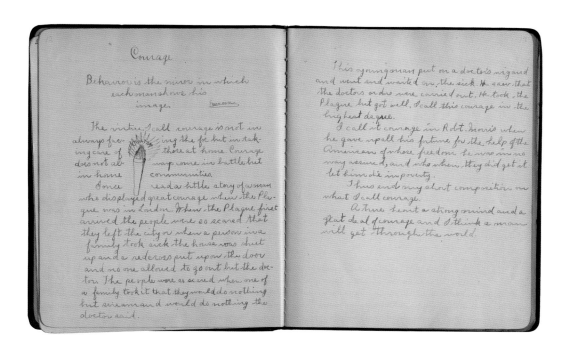

Grade School

As with Truman, writing was an important part of these future Presidents' learning experience. For example, shortly after the death of his younger brother Arthur, Richard Nixon wrote an autobiographical essay about his childhood and his ambitions for the future. In it he wrote, "One of the things that made an impression on me was the death of my younger brother Arthur." Richard continued writing: "He was very well liked by everybody [,] having a happy spirit."

above
Richard Nixon (far right, first row), first grade, Yorba Linda, California, 1919
Courtesy of the Richard Nixon Library and Birthplace

Richard Nixon.   Oct 29, 1925
East Whittier   Eighth Grade

Autobiography

I was born on January the
ninth, nineteen thirteen in the
town of Yorba Linda California
The house that I was born in
was a big two story building
situated in the southwest part
of town. It had a large fire
place in it. An irrigation canal
that was used in watering the
nearby ranches ran close by
the house. The ranch of about
fourteen acres consisted of
lemons, oranges, and also de-
icious trees such as apples, pears
plums, peaches, apricots. And a
few others

One of the times of the year
that I looked forward to was
the time that the cover-
crop was sown, and had reach-
ed its full hieght. Our neighbor

from our old home to East
Whittier. It was a very big
change but I liked it very
much.

I have attended three schools
Yorba Linda, Sunnyside, and East
Whittier. In my first four years
I went to Yorba Linda School.
My next three years I
went to East Whittier. In the
last six months of my seventh
year I went to a nother school
between Elrum and Bakersfield.
I then started my eighth year
at East Whittier. The subjects
that I enjoyed the most are
History and Geography. I also
like debate. One of my best
chums at school was a boy
named Paul Herbert. We had
some fine times together.

One event that made a
impression on me was the
Death of my youngest

brother Aerthur. He was born
in nineteen eighteen at Yorba
Linda. He was seven years old
when he died. He was very
well liked by everybody
having a happy spirit. The cause
of his death is not known
but it is generally consider
that it was caused by Tuber-
culosis of the brain.

One of the things that I like
to do, better than anything
else is to read a good book,
book, magazine or a paper. I also
like music pretty well.

My plans for the future if I
could carry them out are to finish
Whittier High School, and also
and to take a postgraduate
work a Columbia University
New York. I would also like to
visit Europe. I would like to
study law, and enter Politics
for an occupation so that I might
be able to do some good to the people.

Grade School

John F. Kennedy, second of nine children, was born on Beals Street, a block away from Edward Devotion School. John attended Edward Devotion when he was about four years old. Rose Kennedy noted the health of her children on cards and on John's card his mother listed some of his childhood diseases. His Edward Devotion school records show that John was present only 23 days out of the 88-day term.

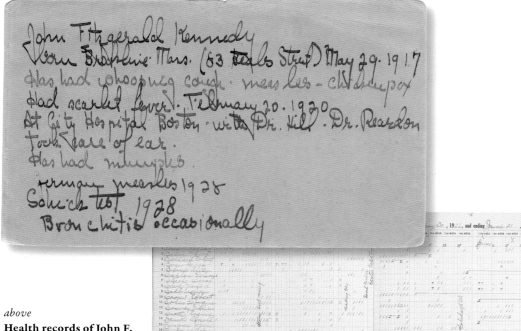

above

Health records of John F. Kennedy, written by his mother, Rose Kennedy, 1917–28
John F. Kennedy Presidential Library and Museum

right

John F. Kennedy's kindergarten attendance records, Edward Devotion School, Brookline, Massachusetts, 1922
John F. Kennedy Presidential Library and Museum

above
John F. Kennedy (sitting in the middle of the first row), Riverdale Country Day School, Bronxville, New York, ca. 1927–28
Photograph by Arthur Studios, John F. Kennedy Library and Museum

right
John F. Kennedy's report card, Canterbury School, New Milford, Connecticut, December 1930
John F. Kennedy Presidential Library and Museum

CANTERBURY SCHOOL
NEW MILFORD, CONNECTICUT

Record of John Kennedy, Form II

From November 1 to December 6, 1930.

Any average from 90% to 100% is accounted "Very Good"; from 80% to 90% "Good"; from 70% to 80% "Fair"; from 60% to 70% "Poor"; and below 60% "Unsatisfactory".

SUBJECT	DAILY WORK	EFFORT AND APPLICATION	FORM AVERAGE
English II	86	Good	71.69
Latin II	55	Poor	64.35
History II	77	Good	67.00
Mathematics II	95	Good	61.69
Science II	72	Good	66.62
Religion II	75	Fair	78.46
AVERAGE: 77.00			

This report is not quite so good as the last one. The damage was done chiefly by "Poor" effort in Latin, in which Jack got a mark of 55. He can do better than this. In fact, his average should be well in the 80's.

N.H.

(handwritten manuscript pages — pages 9, 10, and 1 of "Francis the First")

Rose and Joseph Kennedy enrolled their son John at Canterbury School from 1930–31, an exclusive Catholic Academy in Milford, Connecticut. While there, John wrote a report on Francis the First. The first page is written in French.

above and right
"Francis the First," written by John F. Kennedy, ca. 1930, pages 1, 9, 10
John F. Kennedy Presidential Library and Museum

Rebekah Johnson taught her son Lyndon the
alphabet by the age of three. At four he could read
and followed his cousins to the local elementary
school to sit in on the classes. Lyndon began his
formal schooling in first grade when he attended the
Johnson City School.

above
**Lyndon B. Johnson's
third grade report card,
Johnson City, Texas, 1917**
*Courtesy of the Collection of
Johnson City Foundation*

After George H.W. Bush graduated from Yale, he moved his family to Texas. His oldest child, George W. Bush, was three years old when they moved.

Grade School

above

Gerald R. Ford, Madison Elementary School, Grand Rapids, Michigan, ca. 1923

Gerald R. Ford Presidential Library and Museum

above

George W. Bush with his father George H.W. Bush, March 20, 1956

George H.W. Bush Presidential Library and Museum

right

George W. Bush's first grade report card, Sam Houston Elementary School, Midland, Texas, 1952–53

George H.W. Bush Presidential Library and Museum

MIDLAND PUBLIC SCHOOLS

Sam Houston Elem.

195_2_ to 195_3_

PUPIL'S REPORT CARD

Report of Bush, George W.

Grade 1   Teacher Miss Kearns

1. GRADE VALUES:
   A is excellent; B is good; C is fair; D is poor; F is failure.
2. CITIZENSHIP VALUES:
   E is excellent; G is good; F is fair; P is poor; VP is very poor.

ACHIEVEMENT IN SUBJECTS BY SIX WEEKS PERIOD

	1	2	3	Ex.	Av.	1	2	3	Ex.	Av.
Language										
Social Studies										
Writing	B	B+	B+	B+		a-	B-	a·		a-
Reading	a	a	a	a		a	a	a		a
Spelling						a	a	a		a
Arithmetic	a	a	a	a		a	a	a		a
Science										
Spanish										
Health Education										
Physical Education										
Music	a	a	a	a		a	a	a·		a
Art	B+	C+	B	B+		a-	B-	a·		a
Citizenship	G	G	G	G		G	G	G		G
Height										
Weight										
Days Absent	1	2	3			0	0	1		
Days Present	29	27	24			30	30	32		
Times Tardy	0	0	01			0	0	0		

Mr. C.B. Downing   PRINCIPAL

"The home and the school should work together for the welfare of the child"

Jimmy Carter grew up in rural Georgia in the 1930s and attended the same school, Plains High School, from 1st through 11th grade.

left
Jimmy Carter, around 10 years old, with his sisters Gloria, age 8, and Ruth, age 5
Jimmy Carter Presidential Library and Museum

above
Bill Clinton (far left) at Miss Mary's Kindergarten, Hope, Arkansas, May 6, 1950
Courtesy of William J. Clinton

High School

"In my childhood a high school education was an exceptional opportunity for an American boy or girl; a college education was possible only to an exceedingly small minority."

Franklin D. Roosevelt

above

Gerald R. Ford's high school record card, South High School, Grand Rapids, Michigan, June 19, 1931

Gerald R. Ford Presidential Library and Museum

High school is an important time for students as they make their transition from child to young adult in a setting of expanding educational and extracurricular experiences. After grade school, some future Presidents attended their local high school, while others went away to boarding school. As their classwork became more varied and demanding, their report cards reveal how well they succeeded with these more challenging courses. Whether their school was large or small, a little-known public school or a well-known private academy, each young man's world of education, sports, and social activities expanded in high school.

ABILENE CITY SCHOOLS
HIGH SCHOOL CREDIT SHEET

PUPIL'S NAME _Dwight Eisenhower_   FILING INITIAL _E_

STUDY	GRADE 1st T	GRADE 2nd T	YEAR	TEXT	TEACHER	REMARKS
English 1	88	88	05-06			
Algebra 1	93	93	05-06			
Latin 1	93	93	05-06			
Physical Geog. 1						
Latin Comp	95	95	05-06			
Rhetoricals	86	86	05-06			
English 2	82+	86	06-07	Johnson Lit	Daisy Martin	Lake Classics
Algebra 2	90-	96	.06	Wentworth	C. H. Brooks	2 yr last half
Latin 2	85+	85	06-07	Caesar	Lavinia Donica	Harper + Tolman
Ancient History 2	88+	88+	06-07	Myers	Pauline Sluth	
Geometry 2	96	97+	07	Philips Fish	C. H. Brooks	First half
German 1	93	93	05-06	Co		
English 3	I	I	07-08	Quackenbos	S. Dickinson	Classics
Geometry 3	I+		07-08	Phillips Fish	M. Picette	
Latin 3	II	II	07-08	Cicero	L. Donica	
German 2						
Botany 1						
Eng. 1 First Class	I+	I+	07-08	Higginson Champ	P. Williams	
			07-08			
English 4	II+	II+	'08-'09	Quackenbos	Lucy Dickinson	Johnson Simonds Classics
Latin 4						
German 3						
Physics 1	I	I+	08-09	C and C	C. H. Kesler	
American History 1	II	II	08-09			
Chemistry 1						
Econ	II+	I	08-09		J. H. R. Spit	

I hereby certify that the above is a true copy of the records in Abilene High School.

Date _____   _____ Principal

left
Harry S. Truman (top row, fourth from the left), senior class, Independence High School, Independence, Missouri, ca. 1901
Harry S. Truman Presidential Library and Museum

above
Dwight D. Eisenhower's high school transcript, Abilene High School, Abilene, Kansas, 1905–09
Courtesy of the Dickenson County Historical Society

High School

Until the age of 14, Franklin Roosevelt was taught by private tutors. When he entered school at Groton, a private academy for the privileged in Massachusetts, it was his first time away from his parents and one of his first experiences in a classroom with other students. At Groton, Franklin met one of his lifelong role models, Endicott Peabody, founder and longtime headmaster of the Groton School.

GROTON SCHOOL,
GROTON, MASS.

Report of *F. Roosevelt* III *form*
for the month ending *Oct 17 - 1896*
Rank in Class of *19* Boys *4*

	MONTHLY AVERAGE.	EXAMINATION MARKS.
Latin,	7.70	
Composition,		
Greek,	6.75	
Composition,		
Mathematics, Trigonometry, Geometry, Algebra, Arithmetic,	9.75	
English, Literature, Composition, Grammar, Reading,	8.50 8.40	
French,	8.00	
German,		
History,	7.33	
Science,	7.50	
Physics,		
Sacred Studies,	8.00	
Punctuality,	10.00	
Neatness,	9.68	
Decorum,		
AVERAGE MARK FOR THE MONTH,	7.79	
AVERAGE MARK FOR THE TERM,		

REMARKS. *Very good. He strikes me as an intelligent & faithful scholar & a good boy.*

E. Peabody

above
Franklin D. Roosevelt's formal portrait, Groton School, 1900
Franklin D. Roosevelt Presidential Library and Museum

left
Franklin D. Roosevelt's Groton School report card, Groton, Massachusetts, October 1896
Franklin D. Roosevelt Presidential Library and Museum

Groton School
Sept 27th '96

Dear Papa and Mama

I am getting on very well so far. Thanks very much for your letters; the more the better.

I have not had any blackmarks or latenesses yet and I am much better in my studies.

I got the best mark in Algebra yesterday this morning and the day before I got the best in English Composition. Yesterday afternoon our 1st eleven we played the Brookline High School team, a lot of toughs, and beat them quite badly, the score was 16 – 0 and for the first game of the season it was very good.

I cheered myself hoarse so that I was quite croaky at choir practice.

I like Greek very much, it is very easy so far, and Mr. Abbott, a young Englishman just come to the school, gives us very short lessons. I am going to try for the punctuality prize, but it will be hard work, as one lateness will spoil.

The Biddle boy is quite crazy, fresh and stupid. he has been boot-boxed once and threatened to be pumped several times. Our 4th twenty-two play four times a week, and we have had some very desperate battles. My head is a little bunged up, but otherwise I am all right. Mr. Peabody read to us in his study several evenings in the week after supper. I eat a great deal and I have gained several pounds.

I am going to Groton on Wednesday for the second time. A number of boys have fruit sent them and it is kept in the fruit closet and given out three or four times a week. Could you send me some grapes or other small fruit? It would be very nice.

With lots of love to Muriel and Warren and papa and yourself
affectionately
Franklin D Roosevelt

Roosevelt, who wrote home daily, had been at Groton for less than a month when he reported, "I have not had any blackmarks or latenesses yet."

Franklin D. Roosevelt's letter home to parents while at Groton, September 27, 1896
Franklin D. Roosevelt Presidential Library and Museum

As an adult, Dwight Eisenhower reflected on his education: "In the fall of 1896, I entered the Lincoln School, little aware that I was starting on a road in formal education which would not terminate until 1929 when I finished courses at the Army's War College in Washington, DC. What I learned at the start would not remain static. In the third of a century between my first and last school was compressed a series of revolutions—political and economic, social and scientific—which were to transform the human environment of the entire globe."

above
Dwight D. Eisenhower (back row, far left), freshman class, Abilene High School, Abilene, Kansas, 1905
Dwight D. Eisenhower Presidential Library and Museum

above

Dwight D. Eisenhower's high school portrait, Abilene High School, Abilene, Kansas, 1909

Dwight D. Eisenhower Presidential Library and Museum

Fifth Annual

National Oratorical Contest

On the Constitution

Orange County
District Six

Brea-Olinda Union High School
March 30, 1928

Program for the Evening Conducted by
PI SIGMA KAPPA
(Public Speaking Club)

THIS year marks the Fifth Annual National Oratorical Contest on the Constitution. Its value from the standpoint of interest in our government, as well as in public speaking, cannot be over-estimated. The district in which this contest is held feels a debt of gratitude to the Los Angeles Times for all that it has done in sponsoring and promoting this work.

The contestants will draw for their places just before the program begins.

JUDGES
(Selected by the Los Angeles Times)

MR. EMERSON SEAR,
General Manager, Pacific Wire Products Co.

VEDA R. WALKER,
Debate Coach, Alhambra High School

PROF. O. D. WOOD,
Formerly President of the Luknow Christian College, India.

Programme

Chairman, Principal I. W. Barnett

Quartette { Pale in the Amber West—Parks
The World is Waiting for the Sunrise—Sieta
William Collins, Melvin McMechan,
Clarence Wise, Adelbert Fiscus

GENERAL TOPIC: "THE DEVELOPMENT OR THE SIGNIFICANCE OF THE CONSTITUTION"

"THE EVER-INCREASING STRENGTH OF THE CONSTITUTION"—Richard Nixon, Fullerton

"THE IDEALS OF THE CONSTITUTION"
Martha Spaulding, Santa Ana

"THE LIVING CONSTITUTION"
Theresa Randol, Anaheim

"THE MODERN SIGNIFICANCE OF THE CONSTITUTION"
Evelyn Parks, Garden Grove

"SOURCES OF THE CONSTITUTION"
Isabel Siracusa, Huntington Beach

"THE DEVELOPMENT OF THE CONSTITUTION"
Winifred Barnett, Brea-Olinda

"THE RELATIONSHIP BETWEEN THE INDIVIDUAL AND THE CONSTITUTION"—Earl Lyon, Orange

Pale Moon .... Logan
Out of the Dusk to You .... Lee
Luelle Coggeshall, Mary Hunt, Gwen Pendleton Shaffer,
Nondys Smith, Ethel Peak, Jane Barnett, Georgia Grant,
Laura Merrifield.

Richard Nixon, described as a shy, quiet student, was the Constitutional Oratorical Champion in 1928, 1929, and 1930. He graduated first in his class with honors from Whittier Union High School in 1930.

Program for an oratorical contest, March 30, 1928

Courtesy of the Richard Nixon Library and Birthplace

High school

Gerald Ford was named a member of the National Honor Society in high school, an award that honored students who excelled in both academics and athletics.

left
Gerald R. Ford's graduation portrait, South High School, Michigan, 1931
Gerald R. Ford Presidential Library and Museum

left
Jimmy Carter (on left, holding flag) with Future Farmers of America club, ca. 1940
Jimmy Carter Presidential Library and Museum

SUBJECT	MONTH OF SCHOOL								
	1st	2nd	3rd	4th	5th	6th	7th	8th	9th
Days Due		20	20	20	20	19	20		
Days Present		15	15	18	12	14	15		
Days Absent		5	5	2	8	5	5		
Times Tardy	0	8	8	6	4	6	2		
Agriculture		A	A	A	A+	A+	A+	A+	
Algebra					A+	A+	A+		
Arithmetic									
Civics									
Comp. and Rhet.		A	A-	C+	A-				
Deportment		B	B	A-	A-	A-	B		
Drawing									
Geography									
Grammar									
History		B	A	A	A	A	A		
Lang. Lessons									
Nature Study									
Physiology									
Reading									
Spelling		A	B	A	A				
Writing		B+	A	A	A	A	A		
Latin									
Literature									
Physics									
Chemistry									
Geometry									
Number Work									
Application									
German		A	B	B+	B+	B	B+		
Averages									

ATTITUDE TOWARDS SCHOOL WORK	MONTH OF SCHOOL							
	1st	2nd	3rd	4th	5th	6th	7th	8th
Indolent								
Wastes time								
Work is carelessly done								
Copies; too much help								
Gives up too easily								
Shows improvement								
Very commendable								
RECITATION								
Comes poorly prepared								
Appears not to try								
Seldom does well								
Inattentive								
Promotion in danger								
Capable of doing better								
Work too difficult								
Work shows falling off								
Showing improvement								
Very satisfactory								
CONDUCT								
Restless; inattentive								
Inclined to mischief								
Rude; discourteous								
Annoys others								
Whispers too much								
Shows improvement								
Very good								

B.—This Mark X is placed opposite trait to which attention is called

A—Excellent B—Good
C—Fair D—Ordinary
E—Unsatisfactory

left
Lyndon B. Johnson's ninth grade report card, Johnson City High School, Johnson City, Texas, 1921–22
Courtesy of the Collection of Johnson City Foundation

below
Lyndon B. Johnson (back row, fifth from left), Johnson City High School, Johnson City, Texas, 1924
Lyndon Baines Johnson Presidential Library and Museum

High School

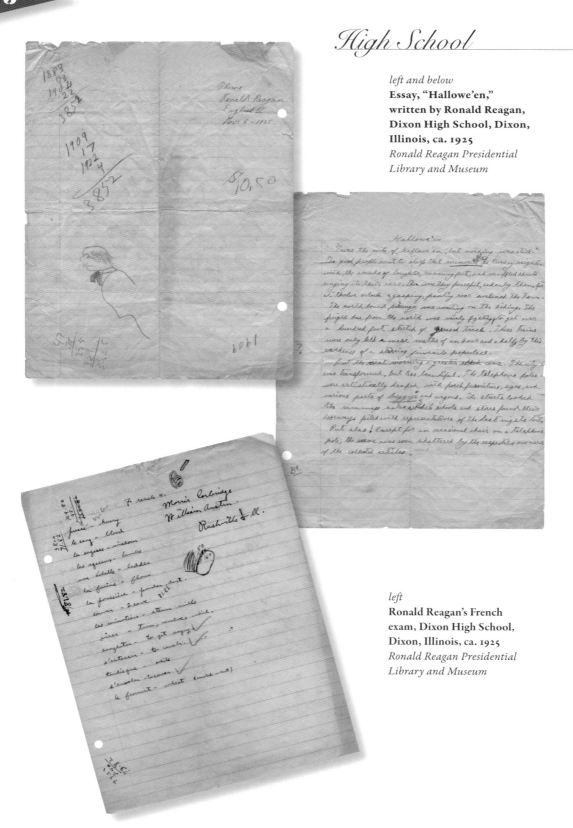

left and below
**Essay, "Hallowe'en,"
written by Ronald Reagan,
Dixon High School, Dixon,
Illinois, ca. 1925**
*Ronald Reagan Presidential
Library and Museum*

left
**Ronald Reagan's French
exam, Dixon High School,
Dixon, Illinois, ca. 1925**
*Ronald Reagan Presidential
Library and Museum*

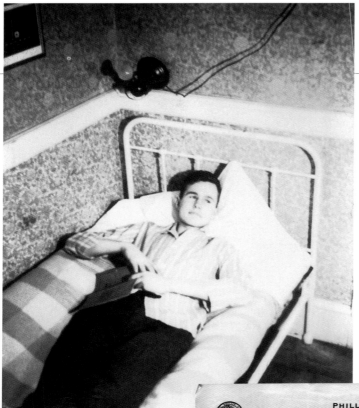

George H.W. Bush attended Phillips Academy, one of the best private schools in the country, in Andover, Massachusetts. On June 12, 1942, just months after the United States entered World War II, George graduated from Phillips. That day he enlisted in the U.S. Navy.

PHILLIPS ACADEMY
ANDOVER, MASSACHUSETTS
RECORDER'S OFFICE

THIS IS TO CERTIFY THAT George Herbert Walker Bush has been a member of this school from Sept. 1937 to date and that the record of his work while in attendance is given below.

Number of weeks of actual instruction in each year, 35. Actual length of the class period, 53 minutes. A double laboratory period is called equivalent to a single recitation period.

The passing mark is 60 and the honor marks are 80 and above.

Grades in brackets, as (70), are approximate for the work done in courses which the student did not complete.

Accredited by New England College Entrance Certificate Board.

COURSE		YEAR	PERIODS A WEEK	GRADE	COURSE	YEAR	PERIODS A WEEK	GRADE
English	1	1937–38	4	75	Mathematics 1	1937–38	5	70
	2	1938–39	3	75	Mathematics 2	1938–39	4	75
	2 (Oral)	1938–39	1	70	Mathematics 3 (Beta) *	1939–40	4	75 55
	3	1939–40	3	60	Mathematics 4 (Gamma)			
	4	1940–41	4	73	Mathematics 6 3 (Beta)	1940–41	4	68
	5 Fall Term	1941–42	3	72	Mathematics 7			
	Public Speaking				Mechanical Drawing	1940–41	2	71 Fall & Winter
French	1	1937–38	4	71	Elementary Science	1938–39	2	75
	2	1938–39	4	68	Biology *	1939–40	4	71 70
	3	1939–40	4	64	Chemistry	1940–41	4	55
	4	1940–41	4	62	Physics Chemistry #	1941–42	3	77 86
					Anthropology			
German	1–2 ** #	1941–42	5	76 80	Art, Studio	1939–40	2	60
	2				Music, Introduction to			
	3				Music			
	4				Astronomy			
Greek	1				Philosophy			
	2				Religion	1938–39	2	78
	3				Social Problems			
					Anatomy & Evolution	1941–42	2	70 Fall Term
Latin	1	1937–38	5	65				
	2	1937–38	4	60	Communications ##	1941–42	1	70
	3	1938–39	5	70	Mathematics S ##	1941–42	4	(75)
	4							
Spanish	1				*Fall and Winter Terms – ill from April 14 to June 13, 1940.			
History	Ancient	1937–38	3	70	**Two years completed in one year.			
	European				##Began during Winter Term – will be completed June 12, 1942			
	English *	1939–40	3	70 75				
	American #	1941–42	5	73 81				
	English	1940–41	3	77 Spring Term				

#Fall & Winter Terms – will be completed June 12, 1942

Date of Graduation.................. Position in his Class for year... Fall Term 59 Winter Term 55 .....Number in the Class...... 214 215

Date... May 25, 1942 ....

Signature... Alice T. Whitney
Recorder

College

"*Everything that has been good in my life began here*"

Ronald Reagan

The 20th-century Presidents grew up in a time when fewer people attended college than today. All of them went to college in some form, from small institution or night school to law school or a service academy. For many of them, college was an extraordinary opportunity and a major step forward in their lives and in their future public service. Just like many students experience today, college was a place where the future Presidents made lifelong friends and started down paths that would lead to important career choices.

College

College

In 1891, Herbert Hoover was a member of the first class of the newly established Stanford University, where he studied geology. His college experience gave him important training which he would later use to become a successful mining engineer.

above
Stanford University surveying squad. Herbert Hoover is on the bottom left, 1893
Herbert Hoover Presidential Library and Museum

above
Photograph taken at the inauguration of President Woodrow Wilson. Eisenhower is sixth from the right in the front row, 1913
Dwight D. Eisenhower Presidential Library and Museum

right
Dwight D. Eisenhower's formal cadet portrait, West Point, 1915
Dwight D. Eisenhower Presidential Library and Museum

Dwight Eisenhower attended West Point. As an adult, he remembered his family's emphasis on education: "From the beginning of our schooling, Mother and Father encouraged us [Eisenhower boys] to go to college. They said constantly, 'Anyone who really wants an education can get it.' But my father, remembering that he didn't become a farmer as his father had hoped, scrupulously refrained from suggesting courses of study."

College

left and below
John F. Kennedy's class notes, Government I, Harvard University, Cambridge, Massachusetts, 1937–38
John F. Kennedy Presidential Library and Museum

right
John F. Kennedy's Harvard transcript, Cambridge, Massachusetts, 1939–40
John F. Kennedy Presidential Library and Museum

THIS BOOK BELONGS TO

John F. Kennedy

Winthrop J-23

CLASS OF *1940*

Government I

HARVARD COÖPERATIVE SOCIETY
· · · *JOIN THE COÖP* · · ·
COÖP PURCHASES PAY DIVIDENDS

President John F. Kennedy's older brother, Joe, announced when he was a young boy that he would be the first Catholic to become President. On the other hand, John F. Kennedy seemed somewhat less ambitious. At Harvard University, he was active in student groups and sports. He worked hard in his history and government classes, but his grades remained only average.

In 1937, John F. Kennedy's father was appointed by President Franklin D. Roosevelt to be U.S. ambassador to Great Britain, and Kennedy became very interested in European politics and world affairs. After a summer visit to England and other countries in Europe, Kennedy returned to Harvard more eager to learn about history and government and to keep up with current events. When he was a senior at Harvard, he wrote his thesis on why Great Britain was unprepared for war with Germany. It was later published as a book called *Why England Slept.*

APPEASEMENT AT MUNICH

(The Inevitable Result of the Slowness of Conversion
of the British Democracy from a Disarmament to a
Rearmament Policy.)

John F. Kennedy
Field of International
Government
March 15, 1940

In this thesis it is proposed to show that most of the
critics have been firing at the wrong target. The
Munich Pact itself should not be the object of criticism
but rather the underlying factors, such as the state
of British opinion and the condition of Britain's
armaments, which made "surrender" inevitable.

To blame one man, such as Baldwin, for the
unpreparedness of British Armaments is illogical and
unfair, given the conditions of Democratic government.

Much of the documentation here presented is of
the type offered in magazine articles and speeches in
the House of Commons. The nature of the subject
necessitates the use of such sources. A wide reading
of the books listed in the bibliography supplied
background for the interpretation of such speeches
and the formation of the author's own conclusions.

PREFACE

This thesis is a study devoted to one phase
of the most controversial subject in modern diplomacy —
the Agreement at Munich.

The word controversial does not fully express
the intensity of the hates and bitternesses that have
colored evaluations of the Pact. This has been due
to the fact that Munich was regarded as decisive in
the battle between Democracy and Fascism. For this
reason many of the political facts and judgments
upon which Munich was founded have been buried by a
cloud of political emotionalism. In the debate that
followed the agreement, especially in America, to
be pro-Munich was to be pro-Hitler and pro-Fascist;
to be anti-Munich was to be pro-Liberal and pro-
Democracy.

Though time and the declaration of the war in
September have alleviated much of the earlier
bitterness, the subject of Munich is still "dynamite".
Upon no other topic, has the ordinary man, as well as
the expert, such strong and intense opinions. Many of
the documents and reports are still secret; until they
are released it is impossible to give the complete story.

above
Pages from John F. Kennedy's manuscript titled "Appeasement of Munich" on which was based his book *Why England Slept*, 1940, title page and preface
John F. Kennedy Presidential Library and Museum

right

**Lyndon B. Johnson's
Southwest Texas Teacher's
College transcript, side 1.
San Marcos, Texas, 1930**

*Lyndon Baines Johnson
Presidential Library and
Museum*

below

**Lyndon B. Johnson's
Teachers Permanent
Certificate, 1930**

*Lyndon Baines Johnson
Presidential Library and
Museum*

Lyndon Johnson attended Southwest Texas Teacher's College (now Texas State University) but was forced to leave in order to save money. He obtained a teaching certificate and taught fifth, sixth, and seventh grades in the small town of Cotulla, Texas. He returned to college the following year and completed his bachelor of science degree in history and education. Johnson later said about his college years, "Here the seeds were planted from which grew my firm conviction that for the individual, education is the path to achievement and fulfillment; for the Nation, it is a path to a society that is not only free but civilized; and for the world, it is the path to peace—for it is education that places reason over force."

College

As he had in high school, Richard Nixon continued to compete in oratorical contests. At Whittier College, he was a member of the Southern Conference Champion Debating Team in 1933 and was the Southern Conference Intercollegiate extemporaneous speaking champion in 1934. Richard Nixon graduated second in his class from Whittier College in 1934 with a major in history and government. He was president of his class in 1930 and vice president of the student body in 1933. He was awarded a scholarship to attend Duke University Law School.

WHAT CAN I BELIEVE

A series of essays prepared by
Richard M. Nixon during his Senior
year of study at Whittier College
during the 1933-1934 school year
in the course "Philosophy of
Christian Reconstruction".

A

WHAT CAN I BELIEVE?

I. How Do I Work?   October 9, 1933

Self analysis must certainly be the most difficult and the most revealing study
that a college student can undertake. Being a supposedly educated senior, I thought
that it would be quite a simple matter to put my beliefs in writing. Upon looking
further into the problem I found that far from being a logically minded college student,
I was completely lost in attempting any close analysis of my ideas and methods. However,
I shall place my ideas about certain philosophical problems before the reader and let
him see what a jumbled mess can be made of a man's brain and ideas by a modern
college education.

The first problem which comes up is the one of method. What method do I use,
or better, what method does my intelligence tell me to use. In making a short study
of English philosophers during the past year I became an intense admirer of David
Hume. Hume's method, more than that of any other philosopher of whom I know was
the most logical, the most scientific. Bacon had described the scientific method but
had not used it. Hobbes and Locke had attempted to work without letting tradition and
preconceived ideas interfere, but they too failed. Hume, however, took absolutely
nothing for granted. He tested all systems of thought by experiment and reason. Therefore, in view of my limited knowledge of methods of thought, I must accept that one which
appears most logical and reasonable to me. The scientific method is the one my experience tells me to use. Taking nothing for granted, arriving at conclusions through
experiment, using these conclusions as the basis for an hypothesis, and then proving
the hypothesis by more experiment! This is my method, the scientific method as near
as I can describe it.

But immediately I find myself confronted with an unanswerable problem. Logic
tells me to take nothing for granted, but what can I do with religion? My starting point
should be something which conforms to the scientific ideal, not a God or a force whose
reality is ascertained by intuition. The true scientist would have no arbitrary starting
point. He would experiment and reason with the purpose of finding one. Years of training
in the home and church have had their effect on my thinking however. My parents,
"fundamental Quakers", had ground into me, with the aid of the church, all the fundamental ideas in their strictest interpretation. The infallibility and literal correctness
of the bible, the miracles, even the whale story, all these I accepted as facts when I
entered college four years ago. Even then I could not forget the admonition to not be
misled by college professors who might be a little too liberal in their views! Many
of those childhood ideas have been destroyed but there are some which I cannot bring
myself to drop. To me, the greatness of the universe is too much for man to explain.
I still believe that God is the creator, the first cause of all that exists. I still believe
that He lives today, in some form, directing the destinies of the cosmos. How can I
reconcile this idea with my scientific method? It is of course an unanswerable question.
However, for the time being I shall accept the solution offered by Kant: that man can
go only so far in his research and explanations; from that point on we must accept God.
What is unknown to man, God knows. I shall use the scientific method to arrive at
what concepts I can; then I shall call that great unknown world, God's world.

- 1 -

Now I am ready to chose an hypothesis with which to work. It is still my firm belief, due perhaps to my early training, that God created the universe as it is. There have been changes in the cosmos, in living creatures, etc., but I still believe that these changes have been within the different "classes" themselves. For example, human beings were created as they are, although their physical and mental beings have changed through the ages! I know that this idea is a laughing stock among competent scholars, but in view of my past education, or lack of education, I can maintain no other theory. Let me hasten to say, however, that this view is not unsusceptible to further development. I am no longer a "seven day-er"! In declaring that God created the world, I am only acknowledging that my own mind is not capable of explaining it in any other way. How God created the world, I do not attempt to say; I am not able to understand that problem. I believe, however, that I should make an attempt to understand as much about the world as I possibly can. With this purpose in mind, I am going to attempt to prove the evolutionary hypothesis. The concept of growth and improvement seems to fit into my scheme of thought exceedingly well. I am not able to say what evolutionary theory I intend to use. What I do wish to do is to give a fair trial to all of them and to either accept or reject them on their merits. Undoubtedly, of course, my concept of God as the creator will interfere with my impartiality, but it is certain that I shall attempt to make that interference as small as possible. God then is my starting point, my great cause or what you will; I shall attempt to use the scientific method in proving an evolutionary hypothesis as to the origin and development of the universe. Certainly, there could be no more jumbled set of ideas than these. Let us hope that further study will unravel some of the crossed threads of my thought!

Finally I am confronted with what to me is the greatest problem of all. What is the purpose of all this study? Where am I heading for? Why not go ahead living and forget this problem of existence? We humans differ from the lower animals in that we are curious about such things. We are never satisfied with just living. We must through know why we live. My purpose in making this study of philosophy is to get a clearer picture of how I came to be on this earth, and to learn what my purpose in life is; I used to accept the biblical account of man's natural depravity and his predestination on to heaven or to hell. My education has taught me that the bible, like all other books, is a work of man and consequently has man made mistakes. Now I desire to find a suitable explanation of man's and the universe's creation, an explanation that will fit not only with my idea of God but also with what my mind tells me is right. I want to know why I am here in order that I may better find my place in life.

With this illogical method, starting point, hypothesis, and purpose, I am entering into the field of philosophy. Where my study will lead I do not know, but certainly any system of ideas would be better than this absurd collection of science, religion and philosophy that I now have!

- 2 -

left and above
Richard Nixon's "What Can I Believe?" essay, Whittier College, Whittier, California, 1933
Richard Nixon Library and Birthplace

right
Richard Nixon's Whittier College grade report, Whittier, California, 1934
Richard Nixon Library and Birthplace

WHITTIER COLLEGE
GRADE REPORT

STUDENT Nixon, Richard

CLASS Senior

REPORT FOR SEMESTER ENDING June 9, 1934

SUBJECTS:

Hist.	202	A
Hist.	110	A
Phil.	138	A
Eng.	14	A
P.E.	82	W
P.E.	72	B
Glee Club		A

A—EXCEPTIONAL
B—SUPERIOR
C—AVERAGE
D—POOR
COND.—CONDITIONED
F—FAILED
P—PASSED WITHOUT GRADE
W—WITHDRAWN

College

From 1931 to 1935 Gerald Ford attended the University of Michigan at Ann Arbor, where he majored in economics and political science. He graduated with a bachelor of arts degree in June 1935. For Mother's Day, Ford sent his mother warm wishes saying his "financial condition" prevented him from sending flowers or candy. Although he received modest assistance from his family, Ford paid for his college education with part-time jobs and a small scholarship from his high school.

above and right
Gerald R. Ford's letter to his mother, Dorothy Ford, wishing her a happy Mother's Day, May 12, 1933
Gerald R. Ford Presidential Library and Museum

above and right

Gerald R. Ford's University of Michigan yearbook, *Michiganensian,* **Ann Arbor, Michigan, 1935**

Gerald R. Ford Presidential Library and Museum

Page 364

Harvey Smith . . . because he spent two years at Illinois where he became the only Michigan man to beat Michigan out of a conference track championship; because he decided to come to Michigan and be a forester and incidentally to show the coaches what a superb track man he was; because the coaching staff persuaded him to come back for another year and be a "master forester" and because he admits to a very few of his close friends that he never would have had such ambitions if it hadn't been for the A.O.Pi president who later decided he spent too much time training for championships; because he's a Phi Gam and incidentally a Michigamua; and because he added an All Conference Medal to his lengthy string of victory charms.

Jerry Ford . . . because the football team chose him as their most valuable player; because he was a good student and got better grades than anyone else on the squad; because he put the D.K.E. house back on a paying basis; because he never smokes, drinks, swears, or tells dirty stories, qualities quite novel among the rest of his fraternity brothers; because he's exceedingly bashful but broke forth the middle of his senior year with a date; because he has decided to coach football at Yale and incidentally to study law; and because he's not a bit fraudulent and we can't find anything really nasty to say about him.

Robert Ward . . . because he's the most locquacious lubricator that we know of; because he was the big gun in the Senior State Street Party (hired airplanes, jackasses and the like) and then after taking a terrific beating persuaded the Washtenaw boys to let him take over their treasurer's job; because he pretends to be a woman hater but has an enviable appeal to the weaker sex; because he took all the available ad writing courses to qualify himself for the Daily job but had to be content with writing ads for Goldman's; because he's the originator of the famous Friday afternoon beer lecturers and can wield two full glasses with with the best of them.

College

Jimmy Carter attended Georgia School of Technology during the summer of 1942 in order to fulfill the admission requirements for the U.S. Naval Academy. Jimmy Carter had dreamed of attending as a boy. In fact, when he was only seven years old, he wrote the Naval Academy requesting the entrance requirements.

Sunday

Dear Mother,

I hope that you had a really happy mother's day, and I wish that I were there with you. I guess that Gloria gave you the ___, but it seems wrong to try to let a box of candy express my love for you. There is no need for telling you that.

I don't think that I have ever realized so fully how lucky I am.

I am sorry that you didn't get this today. I tried to wire some flowers, but all the telegraph companies would accept no more messages. You will forgive me for being late, won't you? I guess you know that I was thinking of you.

I will come home next week-end if it is possible, and right now I don't know of anything which could prevent my coming. I will let you know later just when I will get there.

___ you ___ son, Jimmy

UNITED STATES NAVAL ACADEMY
ANNAPOLIS, MARYLAND

Tues. afternoon

Dear Ma,

I don't know what's the matter, but I haven't heard from you yet, and I've been up here 9 days. I got Daddy's letter yesterday morning, but haven't heard from anybody else but Miss Julia. I would appreciate it very much if all of you would write often. My room number is now 3241 instead of 3315A, so address your letters to my new address.

We go into regimental formation tomorrow, when the trouble really starts. They are supposed to really be strict, but I don't see how. I haven't but a few minutes left, so I'll close. I just wanted you all to know that I want to hear from you.

Love,

above left
Jimmy Carter's letter to his mother, Lillian Carter, from Georgia School of Technology, May 10, 1942
Jimmy Carter Presidential Library and Museum

above right
Jimmy Carter's letter to his mother, Lillian Carter, from United States Naval Academy, July 6, 1943
Jimmy Carter Presidential Library and Museum

Jimmy Carter eventually was accepted to the Naval Academy in Annapolis, Maryland. As an adult, Carter recalled, "The military, West Point, and Annapolis, to us was the ultimate in what a southern young man could achieve. And to get a college education was something that was a dream that very few people realized."

top
Midshipman Jimmy Carter, 1946
Jimmy Carter Presidential Library and Museum

above
Jimmy Carter's Georgia School of Technology report card, Atlanta, Georgia, 1943
Jimmy Carter Presidential Library and Museum

College

George H.W. Bush graduated from Phillips Academy, Andover, Massachusetts, on his 18th birthday, June 12, 1942, with World War II raging on two fronts. That same day, although he had been accepted at Yale University, he enlisted in the U.S. Navy as a seaman second class. He received his wings and commission in June 1943 and was the youngest pilot in the U.S. Navy at that time.

above
George H.W. Bush, U.S. Navy Primary Flight Training, Minnesota, ca. 1942
George H.W. Bush Presidential Library and Museum

right
U.S. Navy pilot George H.W. Bush in the cockpit of an Avenger, ca. 1942
George H.W. Bush Presidential Library and Museum

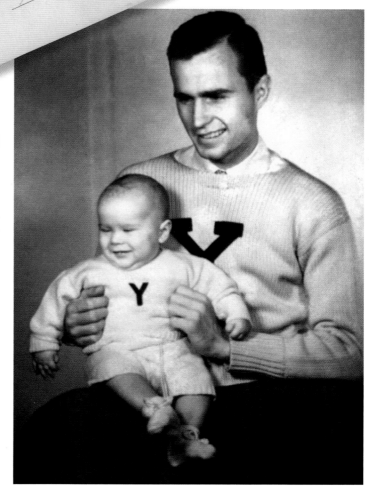

Phi Beta Kappa

Founded December 5, 1776

This Writing Certifies That

George Herbert Walker Bush

Was made a member of ΦBK by action of the

Alpha of Connecticut at Yale University

in recognition of high attainments in liberal scholarship

In Witness Whereof, the President and the Secretary

of the Chapter have hereunto affixed their signatures

May 15, 1948

President

Secretary

When George H.W. Bush left the Navy after World War II, he entered Yale University, where he pursued a degree in economics. He graduated Phi Beta Kappa in 1948. On January 6, 1945, George H.W. Bush married Barbara Pierce of Rye, New York. Their first son, the future President George W. Bush, was born while his father was a student at Yale.

above

George H.W. Bush's Certificate of Membership to Phi Beta Kappa, Yale University, New Haven, Connecticut, May 15, 1948
George H.W. Bush Presidential Library and Museum

right

George H.W. and George W. Bush in matching Yale jerseys, ca. late 1946
George H.W. Bush Presidential Library and Museum

Men of Many Talents

"And I don't think I would have become President if it hadn't been for school music."

William J. Clinton

left
Bill Clinton in his band uniform, spring 1964
William J. Clinton Presidential Library and Museum

below right
Gerald R. Ford (third from left), age 23, and fellow rangers at the Canyon Station post in Yellowstone National Park, 1936
Gerald R. Ford Presidential Library and Museum

below
Baptist Training Union certificate, 1958
William J. Clinton Presidential Library and Museum

As students, the modern Presidents developed their talents and learned new skills not only inside the classroom but also through enrichment and extracurricular activities. Some of these young men played musical instruments and sang. Others were debaters who competed in regional debate finals or were actors who wrote home excitedly about their first part in a play. The programs, sheet music, and award certificates preserved in the Presidential Libraries show the importance of these activities in the young men's lives. These documents, artifacts, and photographs show the wide interests and varied activities that both revealed and shaped the characters of the future Presidents.

Men of Many Talents

In 1894, between his junior and senior years at Stanford University, Herbert Hoover worked for the U.S. Geological Survey, helping to map the geology near Lake Tahoe. Hoover is listed as the assistant in these geological maps covering Pyramid Peak, California.

left
Geological Atlas of the United States, 1896
National Archives, Records of the United States Geological Survey

In addition to serving as Secretary of the Glee Club, Franklin Roosevelt was also editor-in-chief of the *Harvard Crimson*, the undergraduate newspaper, a member of the Harvard Republican Club, and librarian for the Hasty Pudding Club.

left
Franklin D. Roosevelt in *The Wedding March*, as Uncle Bopaddy (far right), 1900
Franklin D. Roosevelt Presidential Library and Museum

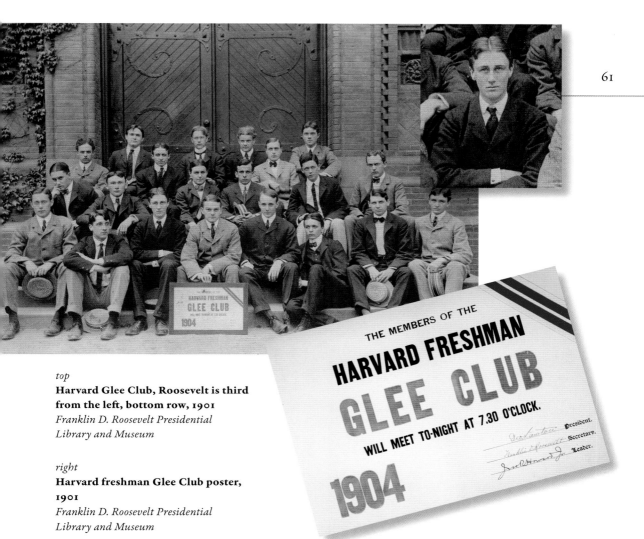

THE MEMBERS OF THE
HARVARD FRESHMAN
GLEE CLUB
WILL MEET TO-NIGHT AT 7.30 O'CLOCK.
1904
President.
Secretary.
Leader.

top
Harvard Glee Club, Roosevelt is third from the left, bottom row, 1901
Franklin D. Roosevelt Presidential Library and Museum

right
Harvard freshman Glee Club poster, 1901
Franklin D. Roosevelt Presidential Library and Museum

28-283

GROTON SCHOOL,
GROTON, MASS.

Sunday.
Feb. 21ᵗ

My darling Mama and Papa
Joyful news! I have a part in the play at last and entirely by accident. Jimmy Jackson had the part of the old hayseed countrified uncle of the bride. He is sick in Boston with rheumatic fever & water on the knee so wont be back again this term. I suppose it is criminal to rejoice but I cant help it! I've got his part, and it's one of the best in the play!!!! I have begun to learn it hard and shall have to work hard as the play is only ten days off. We have had 3 rehearsals last week & I did well I think, tho' I dont know my part yet. Remember, dont breathe a word to anyone yet, till the play bills are out, & I will try to send you one this week.

All your letters of the

Excited about acquiring his role at the last minute in the school play, *The Wedding March*, Franklin wrote immediately to give his parents the news.

left
Franklin D. Roosevelt's letter home to parents while at Groton, February 11, 1900
Franklin D. Roosevelt Presidential Library and Museum

Harry Truman began taking piano lessons when he was about 12 years old, and he probably continued taking them for several years, until he had to go to work to help support his struggling family. He was a serious student and liked serious music. He could play some of his favorite Mozart and Chopin pieces all his life.

above and right
Frederick Chopin's Works,
© **1880**
*Harry S. Truman
Presidential Library and
Museum*

The High School Department
OF THE
Johnson City Public School
ASSISTED BY MRS. S. E. JOHNSON
PRESENTS THE PLAY
"An Old Fashioned Mother"
THURSDAY NIGHT, MAY 3RD, 1923.

CAST OF CHARACTERS.

Deborah Underhill .... A Mother in Israel
        Annie Rae Ottmers.
Widder Bill Pindle.......... Leader of the Choir
        Georgia Cammack.
Miss Lowizy Loviny Custard .... Plain Sewing and Gossip
        Louise Casparis.
Isabel Simpscott.......... The Village Belle
        Kittie Clyde Ross.
Gloriana Perkins .... As Good as Gold
        Margaret Johnson.
Sukey Pindle
John Underhill........ John Underhill .... The Prodigal Son
        Lyndon Johnson.
Charley Underhill.......... The Elder Brother
        Garland Galloway.
Brother Jonah Quackenbush.......A Whited Sepulchre
        John Dollahite.
Jeremiah Gosling, "Jerry".......... A Merry Heart
        Truman Fawcett.
Enoch Rone .... An Outcast and a Wanderer
        Cecil Redford.
Quintus Todd.......... The County Sheriff
        Charley Hunnicutt.
        The Village Choir.

Time: Twenty years ago. Place: The villton in Northern New York.

SYNOPSIS.

ACT I—Settin' Room at the Underhill Fa...
afternoon in late March. The Good Samarit...

ACT II—Same scene, three years later,
noon. A Mother's Love.

ACT III—Same scene, two years late...
autumn. The Prodigal Son.

ADMISSION, 15C AND 25C...

Lyndon Johnson played John Underhill, the prodigal son, in the Johnson City High School senior play. An unenthusiastic student, Johnson nonetheless enjoyed such extracurricular activities as the debating club.

left
Program from *An Old Fashioned Mother*, 1923
Lyndon Baines Johnson Presidential Library and Museum

"PHILIP GOES FORTH"
BY GEORGE KELLY

PRESENTED BY THE ASSOCIATED WOMEN
STUDENTS OF WHITTIER COLLEGE.

ACT I   —AN UPSTAIRS SITTING ROOM
IN THE HOME OF MRS. RANDOLPH IN A
CITY 500 MILES FROM NEW YORK ON AN
AFTERNOON IN MAY.

ACT II   —IN NEW YORK SIX MONTHS
LATER — THE COMMON ROOM AT MRS.
FERRIS' ON A FRIDAY AFTERNOON IN
NOVEMBER.

ACT III   —SAME, THE FOLLOWING EVEN-
ING AT 6:30.

THE CAST
PHILIP .... RICHARD HARRIS
CYNTHIA .... RUTH JOHNS
MRS RANDOLPH .... LEONA OTT
EDNA .... NORMA ALLEN
MRS OLIVER MARY ELEANOR HOLLOWELL
MR. ELDRIDGE .... RICHARD NIXON

MR. HAINES
MISS KRAIL
TIPPY SHRONK
HAZEL
MRS FERRIS
BASSET

HARRY SIMMONS
CAROL ALTPETER
JACK SWAIN
BARBARA TODD
JANE WALSH
PAUL SCALLY

PRODUCTION STAFF
DIRECTOR .... PROF. KNOX
PRODUCTION MGR.
STAGE MGR. .... MARJORIE HILDRETH
BUSINESS MGR. .... HAYDEN ALMENDINGER
COSTUMES .... LANDIS PERRY
PROPERTIES .... GEORGIA AKARD
SETS .... BOB COLE, HAYDEN ALMENDINGER
MAKE-UP BARBARA REESE, RICHARD HARRIS .... BILL MOREHEAD
ELECTRICIAN .... CRESTON HAROISE
ASSISTANT .... ART NICHOLS
STAGE CREW EMMERSON STANLEY, ROBBE
MC WILLIAMS, GLENN TIMMERMAN.
ACKNOWLEDGMENTS
TO THE EMPORIUM

Richard Nixon enjoyed acting and was known in college for his character roles. He later met Pat, his future wife, when they were both cast in *The Dark Tower*.

PHILIP .... RICHARD HARRIS
CYNTHIA .... RUTH JOHNS
MRS RANDOLPH .... LEONA OTT
EDNA .... NORMA ALLEN
MRS OLIVER MARY ELEANOR HOLLOWELL
MR. ELDRIDGE .... RICHARD NIXON

above
Program from *Philip Goes Forth*, 1933–34 season
Courtesy of the Richard Nixon Library and Birthplace

Men of Many Talents

Gerald Ford is the only President to have
earned the rank of Eagle Scout in the Boy
Scouts. These Boy Scout award cards show
the merit badges he earned, including for first
aid, forestry, and animal husbandry.

left
**Boy Scout Award cards,
1925–27, Grand Rapids,
Michigan**
*Gerald R. Ford Presidential
Library and Museum*

right
**Gerald R. Ford (first on
left), age 16, with the Eagle
Scout Guard of Honor
at Mackinac Island State
Park, Michigan, August
1929**
*Gerald R. Ford Presidential
Library and Museum*

THIS IS TO CERTIFY THAT

Gerald Ford

IS A MEMBER OF

Delta Kappa Epsilon Fraternity,

HAVING BEEN DULY AND REGULARLY ELECTED THERETO
AND INITIATED THEREIN BY___Omicron___
CHAPTER OF DELTA KAPPA EPSILON ON THE___7th___
DAY OF___May___, 1932
IN WITNESS WHEREOF THE COUNCIL OF DELTA KAPPA
EPSILON HAS HEREUNTO CAUSED THIS CERTIFICATE TO BE
SIGNED AND SEALED BY ITS PRESIDENT AND SECRETARY THIS
___20th___ DAY OF___May___, 1932

(SEAL)

_____
President of Delta Kappa Epsilon.

ATTEST:

_____
Secretary of the Council of Delta Kappa Epsilon.

"TRANSLATION"

left
**Delta Kappa Epsilon
certificate, May 2, 1932**
*Gerald R. Ford Presidential
Library and Museum*

below
**High school advertisement,
souvenir program of the
Union High School vs.
South High School football
game, November 27, 1930**
*Gerald R. Ford Presidential
Library and Museum*

At the University of Michigan, Gerald Ford
joined the Delta Kappa Epsilon fraternity.
Unable to pay for room and board, Ford lived
at the fraternity house, where he worked as a
dishwasher to pay his rent. As captain of his
high school football team, Gerald Ford was
asked to model in this advertisement.

UNION — vs. — SOUTH

THANKSGIVING
DAY

The popular Captains of
these two Football Teams
—wearing—

UNIVERSITY
STYLES
by
LEARBURY

GERALD FORD   TED BURGESS

*Ted Burgess, Captain of Union High, is a member of
The Varsity Club, his third year playing on the team and
first year as Captain . . . . Gerald Ford is a member of
The Varsity Club, Latin Club, and Track Team and first
year as Captain of South High.*

These models, together with other styles of suits
and overcoats, tailored and styled by "Learbury,"
may be seen at our store. These garments are styled
to meet the demands of the young men and are
always correct.

MAY WE SHOW YOU?

HOUSEMAN & JONES
79 Years a Grand Rapids Institution

George and Barbara Bush met at a country club dance in Connecticut during Christmas break in 1941. She was a 16-year-old student at a Charleston, South Carolina, prep school. He was a senior at Phillips Academy in Andover, Massachusetts. When they returned to their schools, they kept in touch by writing letters. In a letter from 1942, Barbara accepted Poppy's (his nickname) invitation to the Phillips Academy Promenade.

below

Letter from Barbara Pierce (Bush) to Poppy (George H.W. Bush), Charleston, South Carolina, 1942

George H.W. Bush Presidential Library and Museum

Charleston, S. C.

Ashley Hall

Barbara Pierce

Friday—

Dear Poppy—
I think it was perfectly swell of you to invite me to the dance and I would love to come or go or whatever you say. I wrote him yesterday or the day before and, rather logically, I haven't heard from her, BUT I'm sure she is going to let me come or go, etc. I really am excited, but scared to death, too. If you hear a big noise up there, don't worry, it's just my knees knocking.

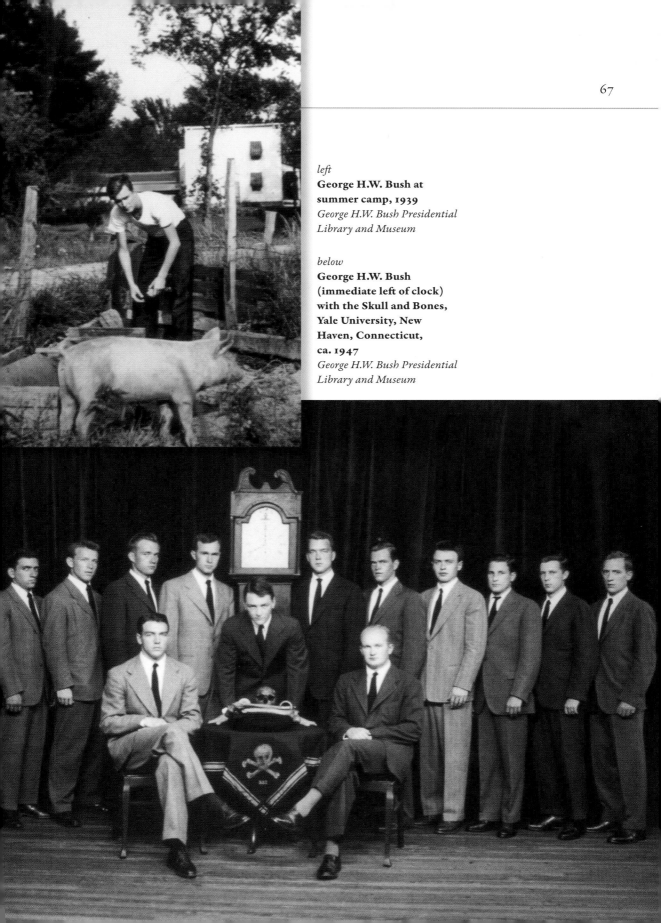

left

George H.W. Bush at summer camp, 1939
George H.W. Bush Presidential Library and Museum

below

George H.W. Bush (immediate left of clock) with the Skull and Bones, Yale University, New Haven, Connecticut, ca. 1947
George H.W. Bush Presidential Library and Museum

Men of Many Talents

At Hot Springs High School, the music teacher and band director, Virgil Spurlin, selected Bill Clinton to be the band major. In addition to playing in the school marching band, Bill played the saxophone in the Stardusters, the school's dance band.

left
Music Stand, Stardusters Jazz Band from Hot Springs High School, ca. 1964
William J. Clinton Presidential Library and Museum

left
Bill Clinton holding his saxophone at home, Hot Springs, Arkansas, August 19, 1958
William J. Clinton Presidential Library and Museum

United States Senate
COMMITTEE ON FOREIGN RELATIONS

July 25, 1963

Mr. and Mrs. Roger M. Clinton
213 Scully Street
Hot Springs, Arkansas

Dear Mr. and Mrs. Clinton:

Last Monday, Senator McClellan and I had lunch with your son and Larry Taunton when they were here for Boys' Nation.

It was a privilege to be with these boys. Your son is a fine young man, and I am sure you are proud of him. I just want you to know that it was a pleasure to have met him.

With all good wishes, I am

Sincerely yours,

J. W. Fulbright

JWF:kj

While he was still in high school, Bill met Senator J. William Fulbright, a Democratic senator from Arkansas, at Boys Nation. Clinton admired Senator Fulbright and later, while a student at Georgetown University, worked part-time for the Senate Foreign Relations Committee, which was headed by Fulbright. The senator was influential in guiding Clinton in his early political career.

above
Letter from Senator Fulbright to Bill Clinton's parents, July 25, 1963
William J. Clinton Presidential Library and Museum

left
Hot Springs High School seniors who were National Merit semifinalists, Bill Clinton (second from right), with Bobby Haness, Pat Brady, Jim McDougal, and Sammy White, Hot Springs, Arkansas, 1963
William J. Clinton Presidential Library and Museum

Men of Many Talents

Ronald Reagan (front row at left, hand on chin) sitting with other caddies for the Lincoln Highway Ladies Golf Tournament, 1922
Ronald Reagan Presidential Library and Museum

A Winning Spirit

"Politics is an astonishing profession – it has … enabled me to go from being an obscure member of the junior varsity at Harvard to being an honorary member of the Football Hall of Fame."

John F. Kennedy

below
Harvard second football team, John F. Kennedy is standing in the second row from the back, third from right, 1937
John F. Kennedy Presidential Library and Museum

below
Jimmy Carter (No. 10) with the Plains High School basketball team, ca. 1939
Jimmy Carter Presidential Library and Museum

bottom
Dixon High School football team (Ronald Reagan is fourth from the left, in the first row), 1925
Ronald Reagan Presidential Library and Museum

Most of the 20th-century Presidents participated enthusiastically in sports throughout their time in school; some of them even got into college based partially upon their sports talents. Most of these future leaders continued their sports interests and participation even when they became President. Whether it was football, baseball, basketball, golf, or the swim team, the dynamics of sports were an important part of each young man's formative years. A few were gifted athletes, but all of them learned sportsmanship and teamwork through athletics.

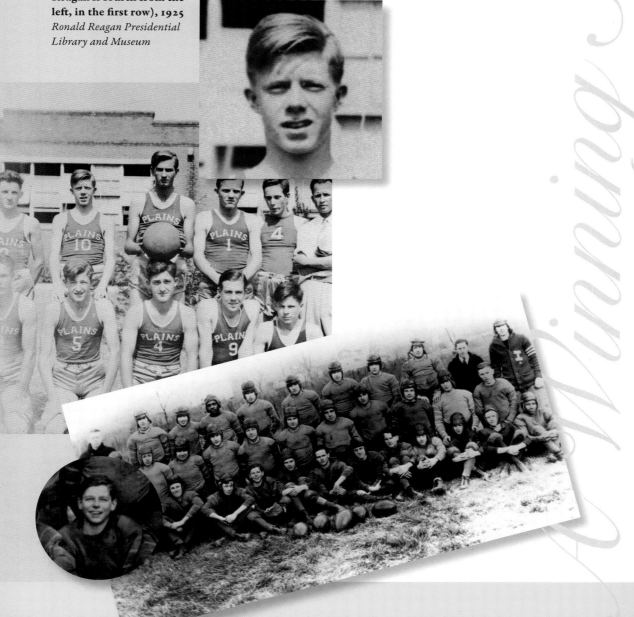

A Winning Spirit

Although not a star athlete himself, Franklin Roosevelt enjoyed participating in and viewing athletic competitions at Harvard. At Harvard football, baseball, and track competitions, Roosevelt would wear a badge in support of his school.

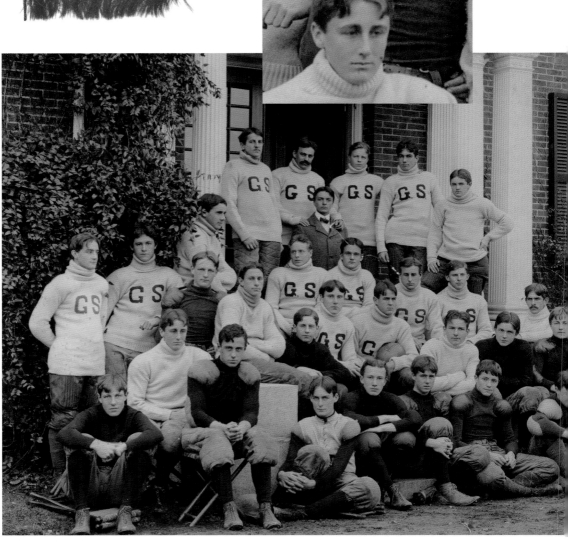

Franklin Roosevelt's first opportunity to participate in team sports was at Groton. In his senior year, he was manager of the baseball team, which, to him, was an important but "thankless task."

below
Franklin D. Roosevelt playing golf at Campobello (while away from school), 1904
Franklin D. Roosevelt Presidential Library and Museum

top left
Harvard University badge, Bowdoin vs. Harvard, September 30, 1903
Franklin D. Roosevelt Presidential Library and Museum

above
Baseball team at Groton (Franklin D. Roosevelt is third from right in the back row), 1899
Franklin D. Roosevelt Presidential Library and Museum

left
Football team at Groton (Franklin D. Roosevelt is second from left, first row), 1899
Franklin D. Roosevelt Presidential Library and Museum

Athletics

By Dwight Eisenhower

EARLY in the fall of 1908, the High School boys organized an Athletic Association for the year. After electing Dwight Eisenhower president, Harry Makins vice-president and Herbert Sommers secretary and treasurer, we proceeded to do business.

Deciding not to play any base ball in the fall, we started on football at once. Bruce Hurd was elected captain, and soon a large number of candidates for the squad were out working. After two weeks of hard work, Captain Hurd decided on the following team:

Left end.............................Huffman
Left tackle.........................Ingersoll
Left guard...........................Pattin
Center................................Funk
Right guard..........................Weckle
Right tackle..........................Hurd
Right end.....................D. Eisenhower
Quarter............................Merrifield
Left half............................Makins
Right half..........................Sommers
Full back......................E. Eisenhower

We were deprived of our coach, but nevertheless, turned out a very creditable team. Unfortunately, however, only four games were played during the season, not giving the team a chance to prove its ability. But for the games that were played, the students supported the team loyally, and time and again the boys surmounted great difficulties, cheered on by the fierce enthusiasm displayed by our rooters.

After the football season closed, we had to spend the winter dreaming of past victories and future glories, for A. H. S. boasts of no indoor gymnasium, and basket ball was never played here. But we improved the condition of the Association itself, by drawing up a constitution, which makes the organization a permanent one, and each year it will be simply a question of electing new officers.

Thanking the citizens of the town who have taken such an interest in the High School Athletics, and also our fellow classmates for their loyalty to us, we are yours for future victories on the gridiron by teams of dear old A. H. S.

FOOTBALL SCHEDULE

Abilene vs. Junction City at Junction City.
Abilene vs. Junction City at Abilene.
Abilene vs. Chapman at Abilene.
Abilene vs. Agricultural College at Abilene.

— THE VAULTER —

Dwight Eisenhower played football and baseball in high school. In 1908 he helped form and was elected president of the Athletic Association, which was responsible for raising funds for the football and baseball teams.

top
Helianthus, Abilene High School yearbook, 1909
Dwight D. Eisenhower Presidential Library and Museum

left
Dwight D. Eisenhower kicking football at West Point, 1912
Dwight D. Eisenhower Presidential Library and Museum

above
**Abilene High School football
team (Dwight D. Eisenhower
is in the back row, third from
left), 1909**
*Dwight D. Eisenhower
Presidential Library and Museum*

A Winning Spirit

Ford was all-city and all-state center in his high school senior year. He later recalled his coach teaching "You play to win . . . but you always play within the rules."

left
Gerald R. Ford's letter sweater from the University of Michigan
Gerald R. Ford Presidential Library and Museum

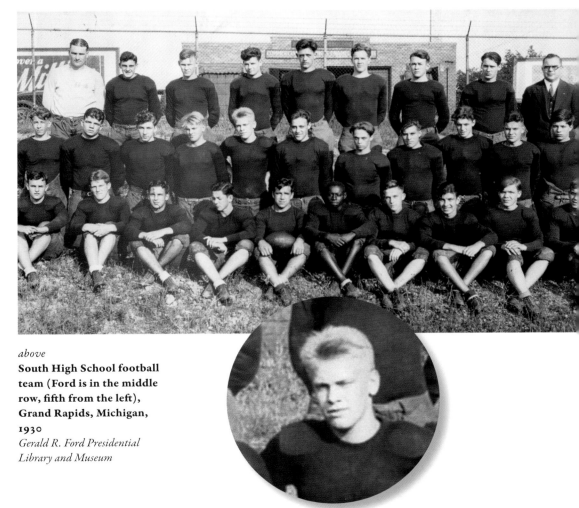

above
South High School football team (Ford is in the middle row, fifth from the left), Grand Rapids, Michigan, 1930
Gerald R. Ford Presidential Library and Museum

GREEN BAY FOOTBALL CORPORATION

"PACKERS"

GREEN BAY, WISCONSIN

Feb. 11, 1935

Gerald Ford
University of Michigan
Ann Arbor, Michigan

Dear Ford:

While on the Coast you told me you were un-
decided in regard to playing professional football.

We plan on signing a center for the coming
season and will pay you $110.00 per game if you wish to join
the "Packers". Our league schedule is not drafted but we usually
play fourteen games. We pay in full after each contest and all
injured players are paid immediately after each game.

Will appreciate an early reply.

With the kindest personal regards, I am

Sincerely,

GREEN BAY FOOTBALL CORPORATION

ELL*GC

left

**Letter from the Green
Bay Football Corporation
to Gerald R. Ford,
February 11, 1935**
*Gerald R. Ford Presidential
Library and Museum*

below

**Gerald R. Ford on the field
at Michigan Stadium at the
University of Michigan,
Ann Arbor, Michigan, 1933**
*Gerald R. Ford Presidential
Library and Museum*

below

**Newspaper Clipping,
"All City Selections," 1930**
*Gerald R. Ford Presidential
Library and Museum*

GERALD FORD
SOUTH
CENTER

1930 All-City Selections

By HEINIE MARTIN

FIRST TEAM	POS	SECOND TEAM
McGee, South	LE	Jablonski, Union
Kauka, Union	LT	Conklin, Ottawa
Burgess, Union	LG	Tarzinski, Catholic
Ford, South	C	Hoeper, Catholic
Van Norman, Ottawa	RG	Yellman, Central
Brown, South	RT	Tuma, Union
Guest, Central	RE	Joslin, South
Elliott, South	QB	I. Groves, Central
Kalasaert, Ottawa	LH	Pierkocki, Union
Heinzelman, South	RH	Thomas, Ottawa
Cook, Union	FB	Kunkle, Creston

HONORABLE MENTION

ENDS—Britt, Ottawa; Johnson and Rinkevich, Union; L. Graves, Central; Cooper, Creston.
TACKLES—Karls, Catholic; Dedinas, Creston; Shuman, Sevilla; Jelenc and Tomaszyn, Tech; Whitney, Central.
GUARDS—Lewis, Ottawa; Ross and Nelson, South; Uzelac and Indelak, Creston; McFall, Union.
CENTERS—Baker, Ottawa; Miller, Union; Hughes, Central.
QUARTERBACKS—Boggalen, Catholic; Deaken, Union; Berg-strom, Creston; Nelson, Tech.
HALFBACKS—Greiko, South; Laphoher, Creston; Scully, Catholic; Thoe, les, Central; Pillinger, Central; Douglas, Ottawa.
FULLBACKS—Kress, Union; Ottawa; Wisconsi, Tech; Purcell, Catholic; Eckstra, South.

A gifted center, Gerald Ford received offers to play
football from two professional football teams, the
Green Bay Packers and the Detroit Lions, after
graduation from the University of Michigan. He chose
instead to take a position as boxing coach and assistant
varsity football coach at Yale, where he hoped to attend
law school. He was admitted to the Law School in the
spring of 1938.

While attending high school at Phillips Academy—known also as Andover after the Massachusetts town where the school is located—George H.W. Bush was captain and first baseman of the baseball team. A gifted athlete, he also played basketball and soccer. As captain of the soccer team, George Bush received a letter of congratulations from his school's headmaster. Bush also played soccer at Yale and was on the co-national championship team in 1945.

PHILLIPS ACADEMY
ANDOVER, MASSACHUSETTS

CLAUDE M. FUESS
HEADMASTER

November 18, 1941

Mr. G. H. Walker Bush
Day 23
Andover, Massachusetts

Dear "Poppy":

I was unavoidably kept away from the soccer dinner on Sunday night, and therefore have had no real opportunity of congratulating you on the success of your team during the past season. It seems to me that you and your associates have been playing clean, hard soccer, and that the results were apparent more and more in each game that you played. You have well maintained the soccer tradition at Phillips Academy, and furthermore have left it for next year in very capable hands.

Cordially yours,

Claude M. Fuess

CMF/C

left
Letter to parents of George H.W. Bush from Phillips Academy headmaster, Claude M. Fuess, regarding the soccer team, November 18, 1941
George H.W. Bush Presidential Library and Museum

below
Student ticket to all athletic contests at Andover, 1941–42
George H.W. Bush Presidential Library and Museum

PHILLIPS ACADEMY ATHLETIC ASSOCIATION

STUDENT'S TICKET

Admit _Geo. W. Bush_
GOOD ONLY TO PERSON ISSUED

TO ALL ATHLETIC CONTESTS AT ANDOVER

EXCEPT ANDOVER-EXETER CONTESTS

ESTABLISHED PRICE 50 CENTS—TAX EXEMPT

174

PHILLIPS ACADEMY
ANDOVER, MASSACHUSETTS

THE ATHLETIC ASSOCIATION ADVISORY BOARD AWARDS THE

Base-Ball **A** TEAM OF 19**42**

TO

G. H. W. Bush, Captain

above

Certificate for Andover Letter in baseball, 1942

George H.W. Bush Presidential Library and Museum

right

George H.W. Bush plays baseball at Phillips Academy, Andover, Massachusetts, ca. 1942

George H.W. Bush Presidential Library and Museum

A Winning Spirit

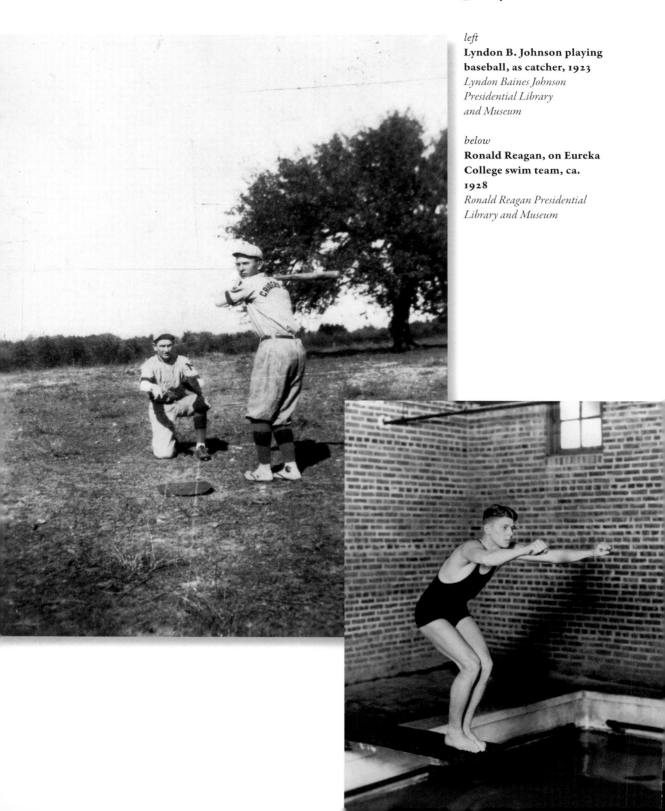

left
Lyndon B. Johnson playing baseball, as catcher, 1923
Lyndon Baines Johnson Presidential Library and Museum

below
Ronald Reagan, on Eureka College swim team, ca. 1928
Ronald Reagan Presidential Library and Museum

above

Harvard swim team (John F. Kennedy is in the back row, third from the left), ca. 1936–37

John F. Kennedy Presidential Library and Museum

right

George H.W. Bush (first on the left, in the first row), Yale Baseball team, 1946

George H.W. Bush Presidential Library and Museum

Bush was also a talented first baseman. While he was on the baseball team at Yale, his team went to the first two College World Series in 1947 and 1948.

Memories

"Iowa, in those years as in these, was filled with days of school—and who does not remember with a glow some gentle woman who with infinite patience and kindness drilled into us those foundations we know today."

Herbert Hoover

"HERBERT HOOVER
The Boy, The Man, The President."

I was Herbert Hoover's Teacher in 1884 and 1885; he was ten years old at that time, was in the Third Grade, advanced to the Fourth during the School year. He was studious and tractable; he had a wonderful Mother, and she it was who laid the foundation in the first ten years of his life that, with his education and self efficiency, made him the great man he is today. I feel the honor that I, as his teacher, may have had a part in guiding his boy-hood; all these things working with God's plan to raise up a man to guide our Nation aright at this critical time.

Herbert was a real boy, loved play, but his lessons came first. I think I never needed to make him do work over, nor did I ever punish him for not having lessons; my school was a bunch of live-wires and something had to be done to entertain them aside from dull Spelling, Arithmetic, and Geography, so every day at a certain period I told them some of the wonders of the world--oil wells were new them, Glaciers were used, which thrilled the boys, especially Herbert.

His home was broken up by the death of his Mother in February, 1885; his Father died in 1880. He lived with his Great Uncle Allan Hoover until August of that year; and his Mother's brother John Minthorn invited him to come to Salem, Oregon, and have a home with his children and be one of his household, and he travelled to the then Far West.

Before he left Iowa, these pupils, thirty-seven of them, decided to visit their School Teacher, and one of them borrowed a team of old mules and a hay wagon and came to my new home in the country to spend the day and have dinner. They came and we all enjoyed the visit, had a dinner that gave unalloyed joy to boys and girls of ten years. That is my last contact with Herbert Hoover as a boy.

He graduated from High School, and his Uncle John said, "Now, Herbert, I have put you through High School; you take one year and go to work; if you make good I will help you through the University." Leland Stanford was just now struggling to life and every one was anxious for a University in the West. John Minthorn was a good man, stern and of strong character, in the real estate business. Herbert went to work in his office; and it was said he was as good as an encyclopedia--if any one wanted to know anything in the business the answer was "Ask Herbert, he knows," and he knew. At the end of the year he had made good, had money in his pocket, but not so with his good Uncle; he had failed, had nothing, and Herbert said "What shall I do, I have no money and few friends? I know what I will do--I know a man who will put me through Leland Stanford; that is Herbert Hoover." And he did it. He graduated in 1895, just ten years from the time he went to school to me he was a graduate mining engineer by his own efforts.

He went to the gold mines up in Grass Valley and Nevada City, California, with his diploma. I have visited this beautiful mountain spot. But Herbert found a diploma does not draw a salary, and so he donned his work clothes and went down into the mines. When some one met him pushing a wheel barrow and said,

Mollie Carran was Herbert Hoover's grade school teacher. In his memoirs, Hoover, who was orphaned at age 9, recalled, "[Mollie] strove to secure me for adoption. But Mollie was then unmarried, and the others insisted that family experience was a first necessity."

left
Mollie Carran article, "Herbert Hoover: The Boy, The Man, The President," 1957, page 1
Herbert Hoover Presidential Library and Museum

below and below right
Franklin D. Roosevelt's birthday card from Endicott Peabody, January 29, 1940, front and back
Franklin D. Roosevelt Presidential Library and Museum

Long after their schooldays were over, these 20th-century Presidents often reflected on their school experiences and the value of education. Memoirs, scrapbooks, and letters reveal the wide range of educational influences that shaped their lives. Many of the Presidents were guided by and fondly recalled a special teacher. Whatever their station in life at the time, wherever in America they were educated, and whatever circumstances they faced, each young man developed a special regard for schooling and the importance of education. These Presidential souvenirs, saved by the Libraries, illustrate what these leaders accomplished, remembered, and valued in the classrooms of their youth.

bottom
Photograph of Endicott Peabody, ca. 1900
Courtesy of the Groton School Archives

Groton Headmaster Endicott Peabody maintained a lifelong friendship with Franklin D. Roosevelt. Not only did he send birthday cards to Franklin every year, Peabody performed the ceremony when FDR and Eleanor married. Peabody attended Roosevelt's inauguration in 1933 and prayed with FDR before the ceremony.

Draft I   4037

THANK YOU MISS GRAY

The demand of the Editor ~~to~~ for a contri-
bution ~~to serve you~~ on the best advice I ever receivdd.
I ~~simply cannot remember any slogan like pieces or
information of that exact sort~~. Perhaps "advice" has
a ~~threating~~ connotation to teen ~~agers~~ which prevents
indelible impressions.

I have, however, met with kindly influences
which shaped my entire things to come. One of them came
~~Was~~ from a really great lady whom we may call Miss Gray.
If I give her real name it can sumon memory and tragedies
which have nought to do with her or one of ~~ff~~ her
missions in life or me either.

At that time I was practicing my profession
of Office ~~By~~ Boy in a business firm in Salem, Oregon.
Miss Gray, by her own devices, made the acquaintance of
teen agers her profession in the town. She gaily and
unobtrusively probed the backgrounds of each of these
working ~~teen agers~~ and their occupations outy of office hours.

above and right
Reader's Digest article,
"Thank you Miss Gray,"
1959, pages 1 and 2
Herbert Hoover Presidential
Library and Museum

-2-

e day early in ~~my day~~ she asked me to accompany her
to the small lending library of the town. There she
ecured a book for herself and also asked for a copy of
cott's Ivanhoe, and suggested to me that I would find it
teresting to read. My reading before this period was
der certain deciplines and was confined to the Bible,
few novels which dealt with the sad outcome of associa-
tions with Demon Rum and the final regeneration of the
hero. There was one exception to this regime which was
reading an inhibited journal, The Youth's Companion,
behind the barn of a boy neighbor's. With my entry into
my then profession my reading had expanded to include
the daily Oregon Statesman when more important officals
in the office finished with it.
I read Ivanhoe. It opened a new world to me.
I liked it so much that I borrowed sequently most of
cott's novels from the library and devoured them in
otherwise idle moments of which there were many in my
profession.

When asked to write about the best advice he had ever received, Herbert Hoover wrote about Miss Jennie Gray. Miss Gray was not one of Herbert's teachers, but through her he learned the value of books beyond textbooks. His Quaker upbringing did not permit much reading beyond the Bible or the encyclopedia, and Miss Gray introduced him to books such as *Ivanhoe* and *David Copperfield*.

Rebelling against the structured life at Choate, John F. Kennedy and several of his friends formed the "Muckers," a term that the headmaster used for boys that did not live up to Choate's standards.

above
John F. Kennedy and fellow "Muckers," ca. 1934
John F. Kennedy Presidential Library and Museum

left
John F. Kennedy's Choate scrapbook, Bronxville, New York, 1933–35
John F. Kennedy Presidential Library and Museum

In his inaugural address, Jimmy Carter drew attention to the influence of one of his teachers by quoting her early in the speech, "As my high school teacher, Miss Julia Coleman, used to say: 'We must adjust to changing times and still hold to unchanging principles.'"

Miss Coleman shaped Jimmy's life. She encouraged him to join the debate team in order to overcome his shyness and learn to articulate his position on issues.

below
Jimmy Carter's inaugural address, January 20, 1977, page 1
Jimmy Carter Presidential Library and Museum

INAUGURAL SPEECH
FOURTH DRAFT

Cor –
This is your draft with only suggested additions as marked. Thought you might need it to ~~make~~ to for your own final editing.

Final draft
JC

FOR MYSELF AND OUR NATION, I WANT TO THANK MY PREDECESSOR FOR ALL HE HAS DONE TO HEAL OUR LAND.

~~IN THE RITUAL WE OBSERVE TODAY, ONCE AGAIN WITH AN~~ *IN THIS* OUTWARD AND PHYSICAL CEREMONY WE ATTEST *once again* TO THE INNER AND SPIRITUAL STRENGTH OF OUR NATION. [~~AS ALWAYS, THIS PASSAGE MARKS THE CONTINUITY OF PAST PROMISES AND THE HOPE FOR NEW BEGINNINGS.~~]

HERE BEFORE ME IS THE BIBLE USED IN THE INAUGURATION OF OUR FIRST PRESIDENT IN 1789, AND I HAVE JUST TAKEN MY OWN OATH OF OFFICE ON THE BIBLE MY MOTHER GAVE ME *a few* ~~MANY~~ YEARS AGO, OPENED TO A TIMELESS ADMONITION FROM THE ANCIENT PROPHET MICAH:

"HE HATH SHOWED THEE, O MAN, WHAT IS GOOD; AND WHAT DOTH THE LORD REQUIRE OF THEE, BUT TO DO JUSTLY, AND TO LOVE MERCY, AND TO WALK HUMBLY WITH THY GOD." (MICAH 6:8)

As my high school teacher, Miss Julia Coleman, used to say, "We must adjust to changing times and still hold to unchanging principles."

left
Julia Coleman, Jimmy Carter's high school teacher, ca. 1930
Jimmy Carter Presidential Library and Museum

below
Julia Coleman and Young Thomas Sheffield, teachers at Plains High School, ca. 1930s
Jimmy Carter Presidential Library and Museum

Graduation

"Education is the cornerstone of our Freedom."

Lyndon B. Johnson

For each future President, graduation represented not only an end to his studies but also a new beginning as each pursued another level of school or began his professional life. This passage also signified the beginning of young adulthood and brought each of them farther along the path to public service and closer to the White House.

left
Dwight D. Eisenhower's Abilene High School diploma, Abilene, Kansas, 1909
Dwight D. Eisenhower Presidential Library and Museum

Graduation

Class Motto:
GIVE TO THE WORLD THE BEST YOU HAVE:
AND THE BEST WILL COME BACK TO YOU

Class Roll:
MARGARETT JOHNSON
JOHN DOLLAHITE
LOUISE CASPARIS
GEORGIA CAMMACK
LYNDON JOHNSON
KITTIE CLYDE ROSS

Class Colors:
OLD ROSE AND WHITE

Class Flower:
PINK ROSE

above and right
**Lyndon B. Johnson's
high school graduation
invitation, 1924**
*Lyndon Baines Johnson
Presidential Library
and Museum*

The Senior Class of
Johnson City High School
requests your presence at the
Commencement Exercises
Sunday evening, May the twenty-fifth
at eight o'clock
High School Auditorium

top left
Portrait of Lyndon B. Johnson, Southwest Texas Teacher's College, San Marcos, Texas, ca. 1927
Lyndon Baines Johnson Presidential Library and Museum

top right
Bill Clinton, 1964
Courtesy of William J. Clinton

right
John F. Kennedy, Harvard University, class of 1940, June 20, 1940
John F. Kennedy Presidential Library and Museum

Graduation

below

Panorama of Ronald Reagan's Eureka College class, ca. 1932
Ronald Reagan Presidential Library and Museum

above

Richard Nixon's Whittier College diploma, Whittier, California, 1934
Courtesy of the Richard Nixon Library and Birthplace

left

George H.W. Bush's Yale diploma, written in Latin, 1948

George H.W. Bush Presidential Library and Museum

left

Graduation, United States Naval Academy, class of 1947, June 5, 1946

Courtesy of the Special Collections and Archives Division, Nimitz Library, U.S. Naval Academy